THE ALEX DE GRASSI FINGERSTYLE GUITAR METHOD

By Alex de Grassi

Publisher: David A. Lusterman
Group Publisher and Editorial Director: Dan Gabel
Editor: Jeffrey Pepper Rodgers
Music Editor and Engraver: Andrew DuBrock, Dan Apczynski
Design and Production: Barbara Summer
Photography (Cover and Interior): Adam Traum

Contents © 2012 Alex de Grassi
Excerpts of "Turning: Turning Back," "Children's Dance," "Deep At Night,"
and "The Monkulator" used courtesy of Imaginary Road Music and Makai Music.

ISBN 978-1-936604-21-0

Printed in the United States of America
All rights reserved.
This book was produced by Stringletter, Inc.
PO Box 767, San Anselmo, CA 94979-0767
(415) 485-6946
www.stringletter.com

Library of Congress Cataloging-in-Publication Data

de Grassi, Alex.
  The Alex de Grassi fingerstyle method / by Alex de Grassi.
     p. cm. -- (Acoustic guitar private lessons)
  ISBN 978-1-936604-21-0
  1. Guitar--Methods. I. Title.
  MT582.D34 2012
  787.87'19368--dc23
                                 2012005700

Contents

Video Lessons & Audio Tracks ... 4
Introduction ... 5
Notation Guide ... 6
The Roots of Fingerstyle Guitar ... 9

Section 1
Instrument Basics ... 11
Fingerstyle Guitar Design ... 12
Holding the Guitar ... 14
Tuning ... 16

Section 2
Basic Technique ... 19
The Picking Hand ... 20
The Fretting Hand ... 26

Section 3
First Phrases ... 33
Note Duration ... 34
Legato Techniques ... 39
Open Strings vs. Fretted Notes ... 46

Section 4
Chords and Arpeggios ... 49
Strummed, Block, and Rolled Chords ... 50
Chord Voicings ... 54
Arpeggios ... 59

Section 5
Rhythms, Patterns, and Accents ... 65
The Alternating Bass ... 66
Enhancing the Alternating Bass ... 69
More Patterns ... 73

Section 6
Texture ... 81
Articulations ... 82
Vibrato ... 86
Pizzicato, Muting, and Harmonics ... 90
Timbre and Dynamics ... 98

Section 7
Moving Up the Fingerboard ... 109
Cross-String Techniques ... 110
Barre Chords and Cross-String Arpeggios ... 116

Section 8
Alternate Tunings ... 125
Voicings, Resonance, Modes, and Harmony ... 126
Texture and Weight ... 132

Section 9
About Time ... 143
Cross-Rhythms ... 144
Arpeggiated Figures, Syncopations, and Accents ... 150
Phrasing ... 158

Section 10
Extended Techniques ... 165
Percussion ... 166
Slapping and Tapping ... 172

Section 11
The 3-D Sound ... 179
Depth of Field ... 180
Orchestration ... 184

Acknowledgments ... 191
About the Author ... 192

Video Lessons & Audio Tracks

The complete set of audio tracks for the musical examples and songs featured in this book, plus accompanying video lessons, are available to download at store.AcousticGuitar.com/ADGMAudio.

PLAYLIST 1
Introduction and Tune-up 1

Section 2
Basic Technique
- The Picking Hand 2
- The Fretting Hand 5

Section 3
First Phrases
- Note Duration 11
- Legato Techniques 19
- Open Strings vs. Fretted Notes 32

Section 4
Chords and Arpeggios
- Strummed, Blocked, and Rolled Chords 37
- Chord Voicings 43
- Arpeggios 49

Section 5
Rhythm, Patterns, and Accents
- The Alternating Bass 58
- Enhancing the Alternating Bass 63
- More Patterns 69

Section 6
Texture
- Articulations 79
- Vibrato 84
- Pizzicato, Muting, and Harmonics 87
- Timbre and Dynamics (Ex. 1–5) 95

PLAYLIST 2

Section 6
Texture
- Timbre and Dynamics (Ex. 6–10) 1

Section 7
Moving Up the Fingerboard
- Cross-String Techniques 6
- Barre Chords and Cross-String Arpeggios . . 15

Section 8
Alternate Tunings
- Dropped D 23
- Open D 24
- D A D G A D 25
- C G D G A D 26
- D A D E A D 27
- D A D G C F 28
- E♭ G D G B♭ D 29
- D A D F G C 30
- D A D G C E♭ 31
- Voicings, Resonance, Modes, and Harmony . . 32
- Texture and Weight 38

Section 9
About Time
- Cross-Rhythms 44
- Arpeggiated Figures, Syncopations, and Accents . 51
- Phrasing 60

Section 10
Extended Techniques
- Percussion 67
- Slapping and Tapping 80

Section 11
The 3-D Sound
- Depth of Field 90
- Orchestration 94

Introduction

I first picked up a guitar when I was 12 years old. I had learned to read music playing trumpet in school bands and orchestras, but I started playing guitar by ear—learning from recordings, from guitar-playing friends—and from the few books I could find on chords and arpeggios. My first guitar had nylon strings, but I quickly switched to steel-string and spent countless hours using the "needle drop" method—endlessly replaying passages from records (yes, vinyl)—learning to fingerpick, note for note, songs by Mississippi John Hurt, Paul Simon, British Isles guitarists Bert Jansch and John Renbourn, and eventually John Fahey and Leo Kottke. Later on I learned a few Bach pieces, studied jazz guitar, and played electric guitar in a garage band. I took some music classes and studied a little classical piano when in college, but I got my degree in geography, not music.

After making a few recordings and becoming a professional performer, I began studying classical guitar and worked my way through much of the Spanish and Latin American repertoire. But I never actually had a "fingerstyle" guitar lesson. I believe many of today's finest fingerstyle players and innovators have learned in a similarly improvised fashion, because until very recently there have been no schools teaching fingerstyle guitar, and there has been very little pedagogy dealing specifically with fingerstyle guitar technique.

This method aims to fill that gap by providing a clearly structured approach to learning fingerstyle guitar that can be used by individuals and in the curricula of emerging fingerstyle guitar programs. There has been an explosion of interest and innovation in acoustic guitar over the past 30 years, particularly with steel-string guitar. The higher tension of steel strings lends itself well to sustain, bending notes, altered tunings, use of open strings, tapping, and a variety of sonorities and techniques that have reshaped what we play and how we play it. Along the way, steel-string guitar technique has been greatly impacted by classical guitar and electric guitar techniques, just as those traditions are now being influenced by the new steel-string repertoire. In the following pages I have tried to draw on all these traditions to present and demonstrate many of the rapidly evolving techniques and idioms that have become a part of today's fingerstyle guitar scene.

This method is intended for use by players spanning a wide range of levels, from those new to fingerstyle guitar to seasoned professionals. The bias is somewhat toward steel-string guitar, because it has been the dominant instrument in my life, but I believe the material will be relevant to players of nylon-string and electric guitars as well. Because this method is organized by topic, and progresses from introductory to advanced techniques, beginners as well as teachers and their beginning/intermediate students will likely find it useful to begin with the first lesson and work through the material sequentially. More advanced players will find this method useful as a reference they can randomly access by topic for the purpose of refining and formalizing their technique, for making new discoveries, and for filling the gaps in their own fingerstyle guitar experience.

The first half of this method teaches the fundamentals needed to get started and learn to play at an intermediate level, and the second part presents more advanced techniques and idioms. Each lesson focuses on a topic with exercises that become progressively more challenging, each one building on the previous exercise. For this reason, I recommend working through the exercises in the order they are presented. At the end of each lesson, there are musical examples of varying levels that integrate and contextualize the techniques covered in the lesson.

Because this method goes into great depth on fingerstyle technique, information regarding the fundamentals of reading music is somewhat limited (though there is a music notation key on page 6). Likewise, I have avoided extensive catalogs of scales and chords. There are many excellent books available on these subjects that can be used as references while studying the material in this book.

As with any evolving form, we may not be able to pin down what, exactly, fingerstyle guitar is, but we seem to know it when we hear it. A lot of that music has been transcribed, and a rapidly expanding repertoire is now available to students, professionals, and amateurs. It is my hope that this book will offer a method and a resource to those studying that repertoire, and perhaps inspire a few to add to it.

Introduction and Tune-Up

Notation Guide

The music in this book is written in standard notation and tablature. Here's how to read it.

Standard Notation

Standard notation is written on a five-line staff. Notes are written in alphabetical order from A to G.

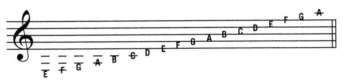

The duration of a note is determined by three things: the note head, stem, and flag. A whole note (o) equals four beats. A half note (𝅗𝅥) is half of that: two beats. A quarter note (♩) equals one beat, an eighth note (♪) equals half of one beat, and a 16th note (𝅘𝅥𝅯) is a quarter beat (there are four 16th notes per beat).

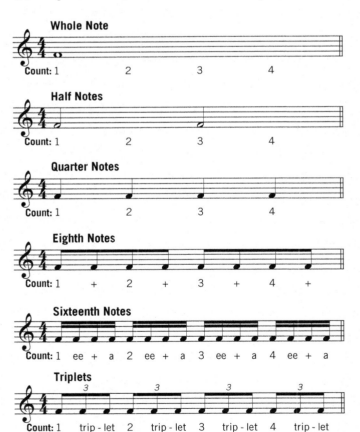

The fraction (4/4, 3/4, 6/8, etc.) or c character shown at the beginning of a piece of music denotes the time signature. The top number tells you how many beats are in each measure, and the bottom number indicates the rhythmic value of each beat (4 equals a quarter note, 8 equals an eighth note, 16 equals a 16th note, and 2 equals a half note). The most common time signature is 4/4, which signifies four quarter notes per measure and is sometimes designated with the symbol c (for common time). The symbol ¢ stands for cut time (2/2). Most songs are either in 4/4 or 3/4.

Tablature

In tablature, the six horizontal lines represent the six strings of the guitar, with the first string on the top and sixth on the bottom. The numbers refer to fret numbers on a given string. The notation and tablature in this book are designed to be used in tandem—refer to the notation to get the rhythmic information and note durations, and refer to the tablature to get the exact locations of the notes on the guitar fingerboard.

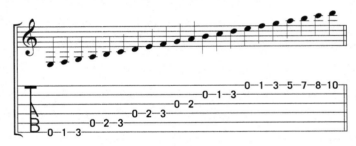

Fingerings

Fingerings are indicated with small numbers and letters in the notation. Fretting-hand fingering is indicated with 1 for the index finger, 2 the middle, 3 the ring, 4 the pinky, and *T* the thumb. Picking-hand fingering is indicated by *i* for the index finger, *m* the middle, *a* the ring, *c* the pinky, and *p* the thumb. Circled numbers indicate the string the note is played on. Remember that the fingerings indicated are only suggestions; if you find a different way that works better for you, use it.

Pick and Strum Direction

In music played with a flatpick, downstrokes (toward the floor) and upstrokes (toward the ceiling) are shown as follows. Slashes in the notation and tablature indicate a strum through the previously played chord.

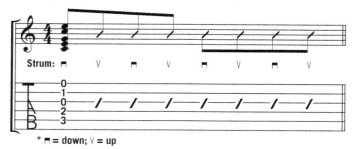

* ⊓ = down; V = up

Chord Diagrams

Chord diagrams show where the fingers go on the fingerboard. Frets are shown horizontally. The thick top line represents the nut. A fret number to the right of a diagram indicates a chord played higher up the neck (in this case the top horizontal line is thin). Strings are shown as vertical lines. The line on the far left represents the sixth (lowest) string, and the line on the far right represents the first (highest) string. Dots show where the fingers go, and thick horizontal lines indicate barres. Numbers above the diagram are left-hand finger numbers, as used in standard notation. Again, the fingerings are only suggestions. An *X* indicates a string that should be muted or not played; 0 indicates an open string.

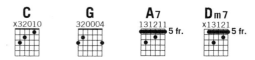

Capos

If a capo is used, a Roman numeral indicates the fret where the capo should be placed. The standard notation and tablature is written as if the capo were the nut of the guitar. For instance, a tune capoed anywhere up the neck and played using key-of-G chord shapes and fingerings will be written in the key of G. Likewise, open strings held down by the capo are written as open strings.

Tunings

Alternate guitar tunings are given from the lowest (sixth) string to the highest (first) string. For instance, D A D G B E indicates standard tuning with the bottom string dropped to D. Standard notation for songs in alternate tunings always reflects the actual pitches of the notes. Arrows underneath tuning notes indicate strings that are altered from standard tuning and whether they are tuned up or down.

Vocal Tunes

Vocal tunes are sometimes written with a fully tabbed-out introduction and a vocal melody with chord diagrams for the rest of the piece. The tab intro is usually your indication of which strum or fingerpicking pattern to use in the rest of the piece. The melody with lyrics underneath is the melody sung by the vocalist. Occasionally, smaller notes are written with the melody to indicate the harmony part sung by another vocalist. These are not to be confused with cue notes, which are small notes that indicate melodies that vary when a section is repeated. Listen to a recording of the piece to get a feel for the guitar accompaniment and to hear the singing if you aren't skilled at reading vocal melodies.

Articulations

There are a number of ways you can articulate a note on the guitar. Notes connected with slurs (not to be confused with ties) in the tablature or standard notation are articulated with either a hammer-on, pull-off, or slide. Lower notes slurred to higher notes are played as hammer-ons; higher notes slurred to lower notes are played as pull-offs. While it's usually obvious that slurred notes are played as hammer-ons or pull-offs, an *H* or *P* is included above the tablature as an extra reminder.

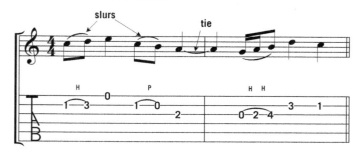

Slides are represented with a dash, and an *S* is included above the tab. A dash preceding a note represents a slide into the note from an indefinite point in the direction of the slide; a dash following a note indicates a slide off of the note to an indefinite point in the direction of the slide. For two slurred notes connected with a slide, you should pick the first note and then slide into the second.

Bends are represented with upward curves, as shown in the next example. Most bends have a specific destination pitch—the number above the bend symbol shows how much the bend raises the string's pitch: ¼ for a slight bend, ½ for a half step, 1 for a whole step.

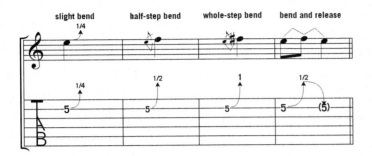

Grace notes are represented by small notes with a dash through the stem in standard notation and with small numbers in the tab. A grace note is a very quick ornament leading into a note, most commonly executed as a hammer-on, pull-off, or slide. In the first example below, pluck the note at the fifth fret on the beat, then quickly hammer onto the seventh fret. The second example is executed as a quick pull-off from the second fret to the open string. In the third example, both notes at the fifth fret are played simultaneously (even though it appears that the fifth fret, fourth string, is to be played by itself), then the seventh fret, fourth string, is quickly hammered.

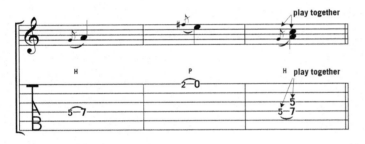

Harmonics

Harmonics are represented by diamond-shaped notes in the standard notation and a small dot next to the tablature numbers. Natural harmonics are indicated with the text "Harmonics" or "Harm." above the tablature. Harmonics articulated with the right hand (often called artificial harmonics) include the text "R.H. Harmonics" or "R.H. Harm." above the tab. Right-hand harmonics are executed by lightly touching the harmonic node (usually 12 frets above the open string or fretted note) with the right-hand index finger and plucking the string with the thumb or ring finger or pick. For extended phrases played with right-hand harmonics, the fretted notes are shown in the tab along with instructions to touch the harmonics 12 frets above the notes.

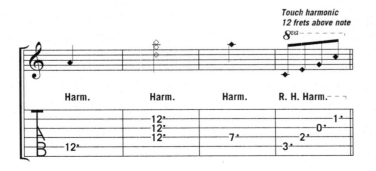

Repeats

One of the most confusing parts of a musical score can be the navigation symbols, such as repeats, *D.S. al Coda, D.C. al Fine, To Coda*, etc. Repeat symbols are placed at the beginning and end of the passage to be repeated.

You should ignore repeat symbols with the dots on the right side the first time you encounter them; when you come to a repeat symbol with dots on the left side, jump back to the previous repeat symbol facing the opposite direction (if there is no previous symbol, go to the beginning of the piece). The next time you come to the repeat symbol, ignore it and keep going unless it includes instructions such as "Repeat three times."

A section will often have a different ending after each repeat. The example below includes a first and a second ending. Play until you hit the repeat symbol, jump back to the previous repeat symbol and play until you reach the bracketed first ending, skip the measures under the bracket and jump immediately to the second ending, and then continue.

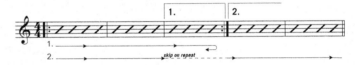

D.S. stands for *dal segno* or "from the sign." When you encounter this indication, jump immediately to the sign (𝄋). *D.S.* is usually accompanied by *al Fine* or *al Coda*. Fine indicates the end of a piece. A coda is a final passage near the end of a piece and is indicated with ⊕. *D.S. al Coda* simply tells you to jump back to the sign and continue on until you are instructed to jump to the coda, indicated with *To Coda* ⊕.

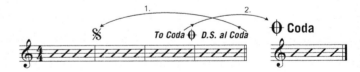

D.C. stands for *da capo* or "from the beginning." Jump to the top of the piece when you encounter this indication.

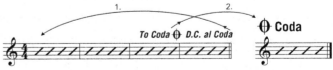

D.C. al Fine tells you to jump to the beginning of a tune and continue until you encounter the *Fine* indicating the end of the piece (ignore the *Fine* the first time through).

The Roots of Fingerstyle Guitar

The term *fingerstyle* is a recent development. When I was a teenager, *fingerpicking* was used to describe the style that utilizes the thumb and individual fingers to pluck the strings of an acoustic guitar. Since then, the many innovations in technique and ongoing cross-fertilization with other styles have resulted in a much broader category that seems to have outgrown the term *fingerpicking*. Today, *fingerstyle* is used to encompass a whole range of contemporary guitar music played with the fingers instead of with a pick.

Long before the term existed, though, pioneering guitarists laid the groundwork of fingerstyle guitar. Before I ever picked up a guitar, country blues masters such as Robert Johnson, Skip James, and Mississippi John Hurt had brought much innovation to fingerstyle guitar through the first half of the 20th century. Big Bill Broonzy, Leadbelly, and Bukka White used slide and bottleneck techniques in combination with fingerpicking. In the '40s and '50s, Merle Travis further developed and popularized the alternating-bass style known today as Travis picking that he used to accompany his unique style of country music. Inspired by Travis as well as other jazz and country pickers, Chet Atkins developed a highly sophisticated, melodic style of fingerpicking.

In the folk realm, the fingerpicking style of Elizabeth Cotten, as heard most famously on "Freight Train," came to be known as Cotten picking and was fundamental in the folk revival of the 1960s. Folk and pop musicians like Paul Simon, Taj Mahal, and James Taylor adapted both blues and Travis picking and built their sound around it. About the same time, the British Isles folk and blues scene developed around the unique fingerstyle techniques of players such as Davey Graham, John Renbourn, Bert Jansch, and Martin Carthy. Many of those players incorporated Celtic and even Renaissance revival music into their arrangements, and they often included solo guitar pieces in their recordings and performances.

Employing the techniques and ideas of country blues players and Travis picking, and using a variety of alternate tunings, John Fahey became, in the 1960s, perhaps the first recording artist to make a career composing, arranging, and performing exclusively instrumental, solo, steel-string guitar music. He was followed closely by the likes of Robbie Basho and Leo Kottke. Since that time, I have been part of a generation of players from all over the world who have participated in the rapid development and innovation of what has become known as contemporary fingerstyle guitar. And now a younger generation of players is continuing to take it in myriad new directions.

At the same time, many guitarists have followed the lead of Andrés Segovia and developed a vital voice for the guitar in classical music. In contrast to the music we call fingerstyle, classical guitar has a well-documented technique, repertoire, and pedagogy taught in many conservatories and universities around the world. However, until the 1950s there were few university or conservatory programs offering instruction in classical guitar. Perhaps we are on the threshold of a similar surge in opportunities to study fingerstyle guitar. There is much to be learned from the classical pedagogy, but the cultural origins, repertoire, and instruments used to play the contemporary fingerstyle repertoire merit their own pedagogy. New rhythms, new sonorities, and new techniques require a new method.

Section 1
Instrument Basics

Fingerstyle Guitar Design 12

Holding the Guitar 14

Tuning 16

Before starting with fundamental technique, let's consider some instrument basics such as guitar design, holding the instrument, and tuning up. Playing a guitar that fits your hands and body, and adopting an ergonomic playing position, optimizes access to the strings and fingerboard and will help you avoid unnecessary stress. Learning to play in tune from the start will make the guitar sound better and sharpen your sense of pitch and harmony. Together, these factors make learning more enjoyable and efficient, allowing you to develop skills more rapidly.

Fingerstyle Guitar Design

It's possible to play fingerstyle on just about any guitar. In the past, players have used everything from small-bodied parlor guitars to big dreadnoughts and jumbos. But with the rapidly evolving techniques and increasing demands of players, luthiers have made many innovations and refinements to both the shape and the sound of the steel-string flattop guitar, and many are now offering a fingerstyle "concert" model. Perhaps the three most important things to consider when choosing a suitable fingerstyle guitar are 1) the design of the neck and fingerboard, 2) a well-balanced sound, and 3) the woods and materials used. It should also feel comfortable to hold and play!

The width and radius of the fingerboard vary at the discretion of the guitar maker. Players often refer to the width of the fingerboard at the nut (the piece of bone or hard plastic on which the strings rest at the end of the neck by the headstock) to have a sense of the fingerboard size. In the past, the fingerboard width of many steel-string guitars has been 1 11/16 inches (42.8 mm) at the nut, but in more recent years most fingerstyle players prefer 1 3/4 inches (44.5 mm) or an even greater width at the nut. This allows the fretting-hand fingers to work the strings independently. The strings become farther apart as they approach the bridge, and are often in the neighborhood of 2 3/8 inches (60.3 mm) or more from the outer edge of the first string to the outer edge of the sixth string.

The radius of the fingerboard defines the amount of curvature in the fingerboard. The larger the radius, the less curvature. Traditional classical guitars usually have flat fingerboards with no radius, but some modern luthiers are building nylon-string guitars with radiused fingerboards. On steel-string guitars, a radius of 16 feet is fairly common, though some fingerstyle players (like me) prefer a slightly flatter fingerboard. The preference will depend on a variety of factors including hand size, experience, and style of play.

The profile of the neck, illustrated as a cross-section at any point of the neck, describes the size and shape of the neck itself. The profile typically has less depth and width at the nut end and gradually gets deeper and wider as it approaches the body, and it has an obvious relationship to the width and radius of the fingerboard itself. The profile can vary from a V shape to a very rounded D shape, with many guitar necks being somewhere in between. These two shapes in conjunction with the depth and width add up to what many players refer to as the "mass" of the neck.

Generally speaking, players with bigger hands will want more mass and depth to the neck profile, and those with smaller hands may want less depth and mass. I prefer a deeper neck with a fair amount of mass so that I do not need to close my fretting hand too much. I find that allowing my hand to stay more open reduces the amount of tension and fatigue, especially with difficult music. As with the width and radius of the fingerboard, players with different size hands, levels of experience, and styles will want to consider comfort and ease of playing as the defining factors in choosing a guitar with the right neck profile.

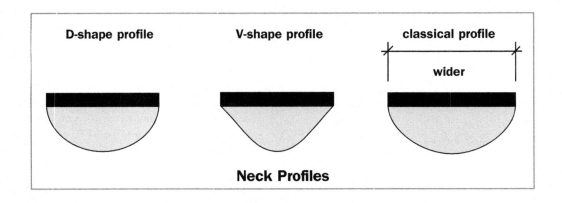

Neck Profiles

INSTRUMENT BASICS
Fingerstyle Guitar Design

In addition to fingerboard and neck design, the shape and size of many so-called fingerstyle flattop guitars have been evolving toward a concert model that is smaller than either a dreadnought or a jumbo guitar. Closer in size to a classical guitar, but typically combined with a 14-fret neck, many contemporary fingerstyle guitars use a shape that's somewhere between Martin's familiar 00 size and a slightly shrunken jumbo shape with a round lower bout and tight waist. This design tends to reduce some of the low midrange without reducing the power of the very lowest notes, resulting in guitars with very good volume and projection, and a more balanced sound throughout the range of the instrument. In any case, players will also want to consider the size and shape of a guitar that is most comfortable to hold and play.

There are many other factors that contribute to the tone, balance, and response time of a guitar, such as the choice of woods and details of construction. Because European and Sitka spruce tops are a little stiffer than cedar and redwood, they are generally capable of more volume, though the tone can take longer to mature. Cedar and redwood are softer woods and are sometimes described as having a sweeter, ready-to-play sound. How the top is braced can also affect the responsiveness of the instrument. The bracing needs to offer structural support, but keeping it as light as possible can make for a guitar that responds rapidly and readily to the player's touch.

There are many tonewoods used for the back and sides. Rosewood, especially Brazilian rosewood, is very dense and is often considered to contribute a rich, dark sound, while woods like maple and mahogany are sometimes considered to have a very clear and bright tone. These features can be combined in a variety of ways to create unique-sounding instruments of similar size and shape. Nevertheless, all these factors are ultimately a matter of personal taste, so there's no one combination that fits all.

Alex de Grassi with his Lowden Signature Model, which has a Sitka spruce top and quilted maple back and sides.

Holding the Guitar

There are many ways to hold the guitar. Guitar players come in all sizes and shapes with unique physical characteristics and proportions. There are, however, some fundamental ergonomic principles that will facilitate playing and help you avoid stress over the long term.

1) The arm of your fretting hand should be able to move unencumbered and allow the hand to easily access the fingerboard. The elbow and arm should not rest on your leg, a chair, or against the side of your body.

2) The forearm should rest lightly on the top of the lower bout of the guitar in such a way as to allow the wrist of the picking hand to be kept relaxed and reasonably straight (see below).

With these principles in mind, the photos show some of the preferred methods of holding the guitar.

Most players find it useful to elevate the neck and fingerboard high enough to allow the fretting arm and hand to access the fingerboard with minimal bending of the wrist. The traditional classical position in **Figure 1** employs a footstool to elevate the left (or fretting-hand side) leg so that the guitar, while resting on that leg, is raised up and angled sufficiently to allow easy access for the fretting hand.

This position has been used successfully by many great players, but some find that the asymmetry creates stress on the back, neck, and shoulders over time. Today, there are many types of guitar supports or cradles that can raise and adjust the angle of the fingerboard without the need for elevating a leg, as illustrated in **Figure 2**. The arms and upper body maintain the same relationship to the guitar as in Figure 1, but these devices allow the player to rest both feet squarely on the ground, thereby helping the player maintain a good postural balance over time. This has become my preferred position.

Figure 1.

Figure 2.

INSTRUMENT BASICS
Holding the Guitar

Some players find that resting the guitar entirely on the right (or picking-hand side) leg (**Figure 3**), with the waist of the guitar straddling the curve of the leg, to be comfortable. This seems to be more successful with kids and, generally speaking, with people who are not long in the torso and those who do not need to bend over the instrument while playing in this position. Some players will even use a footstool in this position to elevate the right leg.

Another option is to sit cross-legged, with the picking-side leg over the other leg, as shown in **Figure 4**. As with the position in Figure 3, the waist of the guitar straddles the picking-side leg. The crossed leg helps elevate the guitar to make the fingerboard more accessible. Note that in Figure 4 (as in Figure 3), the neck is closer to a horizontal position than in Figures 1 and 2, which means the fretting arm tends to hang lower, and one needs to take care to avoid resting the elbow against the body. However, some people may find this position tiresome or even stressful on the back over time.

In more recent years, many fingerstyle players have chosen to stand while playing (see **Figure 5**), particularly while performing. There are many ergonomic benefits to standing, as it allows you to keep both feet on the ground, maintain a good posture, and even move a little as you play, thereby avoiding some of the tension that might build up from prolonged sitting. Standing requires a strap. The strap should attach to an endpin at the butt of the guitar, and to a strap button that is normally placed on the heel of the guitar at the base of the neck (you might need to have an endpin and/or strap button installed on your guitar). The strap should be adjusted to elevate the fingerboard end of the guitar to a degree that allows your fretting arm to hang free of the body, giving the fretting hand easy access to the fingerboard with minimal bending of the wrist.

I've tried all these playing positions in my career. I started out seated with a footstool, went back and forth between standing and sitting cross-legged, and now play seated using a cradle. In addition to being able to sit in a balanced posture with both feet on the floor, the guitar is held in place by the cradle and I can focus all the efforts of my arms and hands on playing the guitar.

And when playing casually for short periods of time, or sitting on the couch, I'll rest it over my right leg as in position 3. All of these positions can alter your picking and fretting hand positions, so it's worth it to try them all and see what works for you.

Figure 3.

Figure 4.

Figure 5.

Tuning

In addition to what has evolved over the years into a standard tuning, there are an endless number of alternate tunings being used by fingerstyle players today. The higher tension of steel strings makes a guitar very well suited to a variety of tunings, as lowering or raising the string's pitch (within limits) still allows the strings to resonate fully. This method will explore alternate tunings in later lessons, but we will begin with standard tuning.

The six strings are numbered 1–6 beginning with the finest and highest pitched string. Remember that the "highest string" refers to the pitch and not the location of the string in vertical space—the highest (or first) string is actually located closest to the floor, and the lowest (or sixth) string is closest to the ceiling.

In standard tuning, the strings are tuned at intervals of a fourth between sequential strings, with the exception of the interval of a major third between the second and third strings.

For tuning, it will be helpful to use an electronic tuner or a tuning fork. There are many tuners available specifically for guitar, and most of those are designed to tune the six individual strings to standard tuning. The tuner will let you know by a meter or colored lights (usually red when out of tune and green when in tune) whether each string is flat or sharp so that you can adjust it accordingly.

It's conventional to tune the fifth or A string first. That's the pitch that bands and orchestras use to make sure all players are

Pitch and Frequency

Musical pitches are identified by their fundamental frequencies. For example, the pitch A of the fifth string of a guitar has a fundamental frequency of 110 hertz. That means the string vibrates 110 times per second when it is activated. As with any musical instrument, in addition to the fundamental pitch A, the vibrating string will produce a series of overtones. These are a series of frequencies with a precise mathematical relationship to the fundamental frequency of 110 hertz, and their relative strength and characteristics give the acoustic guitar its unique sound. The first overtone is an octave above (played at the second fret of the third string) or twice the frequency, making it 220 Hz. The second overtone is a fifth above that, or an octave plus a fifth higher than A (330 Hz) at the fifth string; the third overtone is two octaves (440 Hz) above the open A string; and so on.

Identifying pitches by their frequency is rather cumbersome, but it is sometimes necessary to define which octave of a pitch is being discussed. For example, is a fifth-string A at 110 Hz or the one an octave higher at 220 Hz. To clarify, there is a universal system that assigns all pitches to an octave designated by a number after the letter name of the note. On the piano, the lowest pitched C is C1, and the highest pitched C is C8. The sixth string of a guitar (the lowest pitch of a guitar in standard tuning) is E2. Strings 5–1 are respectively A2, D3, G3, B3, and E4; and C3 is the lowest C note available in standard tuning.

INSTRUMENT BASICS
Tuning

in tune with each other. Tuning forks are used less frequently these days, but they can be a very accurate way to tune. They are normally pitched to an A as well.

As both a practical matter, and for the purpose of training the ear to the subtleties of intonation, it's important to understand how to tune the strings to each other without the use of a tuner. First, tune the A string with a tuner. Then tune the sixth string to the fifth string by playing the note (also an A) at the fifth fret of the sixth string (see diagram). Listen to the note. If the pitch sounds lower than the open fifth string, the sixth string is flat. If it sounds higher than the open A string, it's sharp. Adjust the tuning peg accordingly until the fretted note sounds the same as the open fifth string.

Next, tune the fourth string (D) to the fifth. Fret the fifth string at the fifth fret. Play the open fourth string, and adjust the fourth string accordingly. Tune the third string (G) to the fourth string by fretting the fourth string at the fifth fret and adjusting the third string. Because the interval between the second and third string is a major third, you will need to fret the third string at the fourth fret and tune the second string (B) until it matches. Finally, tune the first string (E) to the second string by fretting the second string at the fifth fret and tuning the first string. The diagram below summarizes this process.

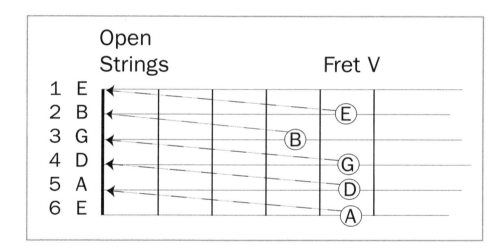

Section 2
Basic Technique

The Picking Hand 20

The Fretting Hand 26

Audio Playlist 1, Tracks 2–10

Learning to position the hands on the strings and fingerboard and coordinate the two together is fundamental to playing guitar. Allowing all the muscles, nerves, and tendons to work together in the most efficient and comfortable manner makes learning easier and avoids the need for correction and relearning later on. In this section we'll look at the mechanics of hands, fingers, and thumbs, as well as getting oriented to first and second positions on the fingerboard. Learning to play simple lines with good tone using the least amount of effort is the primary goal for developing a good basic technique.

The Picking Hand

In this lesson we'll cover basic picking-hand technique: how to position the hand, play rest strokes and free strokes, preload tension on the strings, and get a good tone.

Nails, Flesh, and Fingerpicks

It's possible to play fingerstyle guitar with or without nails. Many players use plastic or metal thumbpicks. Some even use metal (less frequently plastic) fingerpicks—mostly for specialty instruments like dobros, steel-body guitars, and resonator guitars, or to get a particular (steely) sound from their flattop guitar. Other players extend their natural nails with plastic nails or even cut-up Ping-Pong balls!

My personal preference is for nails. I started out recording and performing on steel-string guitar using a plastic thumbpick and my natural fingernails, but I eventually concluded that I could employ a broader range of techniques and coax a broader range of sounds out of the guitar unencumbered by a piece of plastic attached to my thumb.

Many players experiment with applying vitamin E or other substances to strengthen their natural nails. Some find that eating certain foods (like eggs) makes their nails stronger. For a while I kept bowls of uncooked rice around my house, and I would periodically plunge my hand in and work the rice up under the nails to stimulate the blood supply to the cuticles. I think that all these things can help, but I really can't say they helped strengthen my nails significantly.

Most classical guitarists simply cultivate and maintain their natural nails. That works well for nylon strings, but the tension of steel strings makes maintenance challenging, because nails often tear, break, or simply wear down. Some people have nails that are naturally strong enough to stand up to the wear and tear, but many, like myself, need some help. I reinforce my nails with an acrylic coating applied by a manicurist every few weeks. More and more players are doing the same.

Whether you do something to fortify your natural nails or not, it's extremely important to maintain them at an appropriate length and shape, and keep them filed and buffed. These measures not only prevent further damage, but reduce drag and friction as your nail crosses the string, making for a smoother sound and quicker response. I find having the fingernail project very slightly (approx $1/16$ inch or 1.5 mm) beyond the fingertip works well (see photo lower right). If the nail gets much longer, it creates too much drag, and if it's shorter, it becomes difficult to catch the string. I keep the thumbnail considerably longer ($1/4$ inch or 6 mm) so I can accommodate the angle with the strings, because the lower strings are heavier, and also because the thumb sometimes functions like a pick for strumming. I maintain a curved, rounded shape on both thumbnail and fingernails, avoiding letting the leading edge become either too pointed or squared off. I use a series of progressively finer nail files, ending with a buffing file, to smooth them. Fine sandpaper (1600 or higher) used for finishing auto paint jobs is also quite popular.

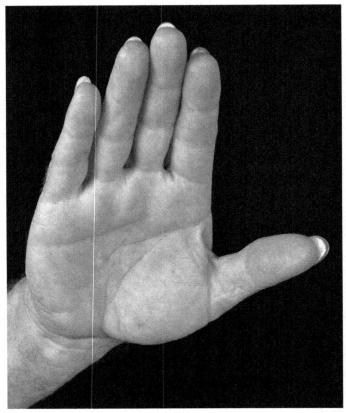

Keep your fingernail length at about $1/16$ inch beyond the fingertip, and $1/4$ inch beyond the tip of your thumb.

BASIC TECHNIQUE
The Picking Hand

I recommend that beginning fingerstyle players let their picking-hand thumbnail and fingernails grow out a bit, but keep them on the short side, and file them very lightly every day using a medium to fine file and a buffing-grade file. If the nails begin to break or crack, trim them back and keep them even shorter. You might want to experiment with a thumbpick, though ultimately, I believe one can attain greater dexterity and speed and a better, more varied tone without it. With time you will have a better idea of what works for you, and you will be able to decide what, if any, modifications to make.

Lever and Hinge

The two fundamental mechanisms used by the picking hand can be described as the *lever* and the *hinge*. The thumb should always be kept straight and move like a lever from the larger joint where it joins the hand. The fingers should be kept curved and hinge at the big knuckle (where the fingers join the hand). These are the two strongest moving parts of the hand, and they should generate most of the picking-hand movement when playing fingerstyle guitar.

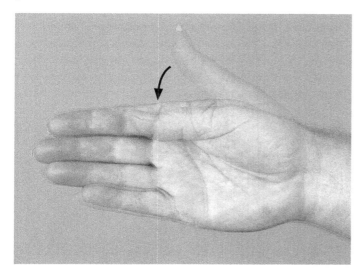

Picking-hand lever motion.

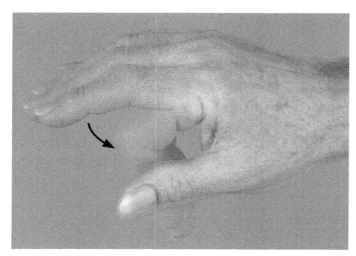

Picking-hand hinge movement.

Hold your hand out in front of you as if you were going to shake someone's hand and practice moving your thumb like a lever, keeping it straight and engaging the large muscles at the base of the thumb and hand to pull the thumb down and then lift it up again. Hold the base of your thumb with your free hand as you depress then raise the lever, so you can feel, as well as see, the movement. Then, keeping the fingers slightly curved and pressed together lightly, move them as a group, hinging off of your knuckles. Place the fingers of the free hand alternatively on the back of your picking hand, and then on the palm side of the knuckles, and feel the movement as your muscles and tendons flex and contract to move the hinge.

The hinge and lever mechanisms not only provide strength; they also define the opposing forces for developing independence of the thumb and fingers, much like the two hands of a pianist. This independence makes it possible to play a bass line with the thumb while using the fingers to play chords and melodies. Recognizing and internalizing the feel of this movement will help in the development of picking-hand strength and coordination.

Placement

Position your picking hand in the area over the soundhole where the fingers can easily reach the strings while you maintain a straight wrist. To achieve this, you will need to find a suitable point at which to rest your forearm on the front and upper edge of the lower bout of the guitar. That point will vary depending on the length of your arm and the size of your guitar, but it is generally somewhere closer to the elbow than the hand. The arm should rest comfortably and be able to move along the edge of the guitar without restriction. Leaning the guitar slightly toward your body may facilitate finding a comfortable position to rest the arm while giving you a better view of the strings and fingerboard.

Position your picking hand over the soundhole where the fingers can easily reach the strings while you maintain a straight wrist.

The letters representing the fingers of the picking hand are derived from the first letters of their Spanish names, as follows:

thumb: *p* (*pulgar*)
index: *i* (*indice*)
middle: *m* (*medio*)
ring: *a* (*anular*)
pinky: *c* (*chico*)

The pinky, or *c* (*chico*), is used by a few players and for specialized techniques, but is not commonly used in fingerstyle playing because it is much shorter and weaker.

While placing the thumb (*p*) on the fourth string, allow the tips of the index (*i*), middle (*m*), and ring (*a*) fingers to rest on the third, second, and first strings respectively. If you have nails, they should be lightly touching the side of the string, while the flesh of the fingertip closest to the nail should rest on top of the string. If you don't have nails, you may find it more useful to place the center or even the palm side of the fingertip on the string to get more purchase.

The thumb should be placed at an angle to the string with the tip pointing toward the fingerboard. The angle will vary somewhat depending on the size and shape of the hand and fingers, but normally the angle would be somewhere between 20 and 45 degrees, with 30 degrees being a good starting point. (If you are using a thumbpick, the thumb will most likely be parallel with the strings.) The fingers should be grouped together and angled back somewhat toward the bridge. They will generally be more perpendicular to the strings than the thumb—maybe somewhere between 45 and 75 degrees—and they will typically be lightly touching each other, but they should not be pressed together so tight as to restrict movement of the individual fingers.

The thumb should be relaxed but straight. The fingers should be curved, with minimal bending at the fingertip joint (distal) and much greater bending at the middle joint and at the knuckle. As you look down at your hand (you may need to lean your head to the side to see), you should see a triangle of space formed by the plane of the strings, the thumb, and the fingers. If there's not much space between these three sides of the triangle, try sliding your thumb toward the fingerboard without moving your fingers to adjust the triangle. The side of the triangle formed by the thumb is often the longest (see photos) but, again, depending on your own unique anatomy, the shape of that triangle will vary. In this position, the thumb and fingers will avoid crashing into each other as they move in opposite directions.

Rest and Free Strokes with the Thumb

With the fingers continuing to rest on the strings, and keeping your thumb straight, press the thumb down (toward the third string) and slightly inward (toward the soundhole) and allow the thumb to come to rest on the third string. This is called a *rest stroke*. Try plucking the fourth string again with the downward motion, but don't press inward this time, and allow your thumb to rise up slightly as it comes off the string so it's clear of the third

The thumb (*p*) and *i*, *m*, and *a* fingers are positioned on the fourth, third, second, and first strings.

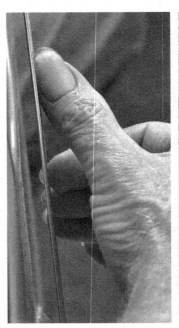

Two views of hand position, from the player's perspective and from the headstock.

string. This is called a *free stroke*. Both strokes should have a smooth, even motion, with the movement initiating at the joint where the thumb joins the hand. This is where the strength lies. Remember to keep your thumb straight, like a lever, and do not let the joint bend as it passes through the string.

Compare the sound of the two strokes. The *rest stroke* tends to have a little more volume and a deeper tone that emphasizes the fundamental pitch. The inward pressure applied with the thumb causes the string to move in a more circular fashion, with greater movement perpendicular to the top of the guitar. This puts more downward pressure on the bridge and "drives" the top a little more. The absence of that inward pressure with the free stroke causes the string to move primarily in the plane parallel to the top, resulting in less downward pressure on the bridge, less volume, and less of the fundamental pitch.

Preloading the String

A sound similar to a rest stroke can be achieved with a free stroke by *preloading* the string just before beginning the stroke. To do this, it is helpful to think of the stroke as having two stages: the preparation, where you place the thumb on the string and press inward with the flesh of the thumb (toward the soundhole) slightly to "load" tension on the string; followed by the stroke itself, where the thumb moves down (toward the ground) and then out and away from the guitar (parallel to the ground) as the nail follows through to pluck the string. Once you learn the technique, the two stages will often feel like one continuous motion, but for now, try it as two separate motions. Press in slightly, pause a second, then follow through with the stroke. After practicing this a few times, try playing the preloaded free stroke with little or no pause in the motion.

Compare the sound of the preloaded free stroke with the rest stroke. Does it have the same volume and depth of tone? When you play a rest stroke very slowly, you may notice that the thumb automatically presses inward, effectively preloading the string before it's released. The inward pressure of both of the strokes brings out the full range of overtones, resulting in greater depth of tone.

With the fingers continuing to rest on the top three strings, place the thumb (*p*) on the fifth string, and try all three strokes—rest, free, and preloaded free stroke. Try it again with *p* on the sixth string. Then, play each in succession in 4/4 time, holding each note for four beats, as notated in **Example 1**.

Ex. 1

Beginning of thumb rest stroke (left) and completion of rest stroke (right).

Beginning of thumb free stroke (left) and completion of free stroke (right).

Rest and Free Strokes with the Fingers

For the fingers, the free stroke is perhaps more versatile than the rest stroke and has the advantage that the fingers do not get delayed or caught up in the strings. Place your thumb and fingers back on the strings with *p* on the fourth string, *i* on the third string, *m* on the second string, and *a* on the first string. Without moving the other fingers, pluck the third string with the *i* finger. The tip and middle joints of the finger will bend, curling in some toward the palm to allow the finger to clear the adjacent fourth string, but try to initiate the movement at the knuckle joint, keeping the hinge analogy in mind. That is where the power lies, and learning to engage the fingers at the knuckle will give you better endurance, volume, speed, and control as you develop your picking-hand technique.

After plucking the third string, place the *i* finger back on the third string, and without removing the other fingers or the thumb, play a free stroke with *m*. Place *m* back on the second string, and without removing the thumb or other fingers, play a free stroke on the first string with *a*. Then place the *a* finger back on the first string.

Play the three notes again as whole notes in 4/4 time as shown in **Example 2**. Count four beats on each note before playing the next note, keeping the beat steady. Focus on giving each note the same volume and tone.

As with the *i* finger, the fingertip and middle joints of the *m* and *a* fingers will curl in some, but try to feel the movement at the knuckle. The *a* finger is anatomically connected with the pinky (fourth finger), so you may find that you will obtain more power and control by pressing the two fingers together lightly and moving them as one.

Play the three strings again; this time prepare each stroke by lightly pressing inward (toward the back of the guitar) on the string with your fingertip to preload the string, and then following through with the free stroke. If the string is consistently buzzing, you may be pressing in too much, or you may need to raise the action of the guitar so the strings are slightly higher above the frets. (This will stop the buzzing and allow you to get the fullest sound from the guitar.)

Now let's try the *rest stroke* with the fingers. Finger rest strokes are primarily used for melodies and scale-like passages where you play more than one note on a single string before moving to an adjacent string. In these situations, it works well to alternate strokes between the *i* and *m* fingers. Place *i* on the second string, *m* on the first string, and *p* on the sixth string. Leave

Ex. 2

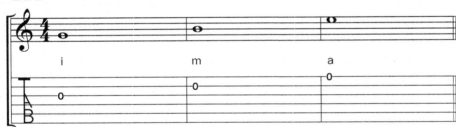

 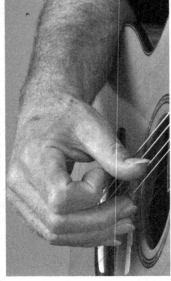

Beginning of finger free stroke (left), and end of finger free stroke (right).

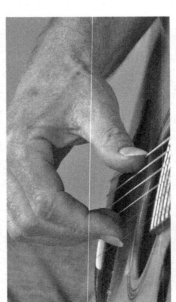 

Beginning of finger rest stroke (left), and end of finger rest stroke (right).

BASIC TECHNIQUE
The Picking Hand

Rest stroke 2

a off the strings for the moment. While maintaining the finger curvature described in the hand placement section above, move the middle finger by "pulling" from the knuckle joint to pluck the first string, allowing the finger to continue until it comes to rest against the second string.

When playing rest strokes with the fingers, take care to avoid bending the fingertip joint of the finger as it passes through the string, because that will dissipate energy and weaken the sound. It may help to think of the individual fingers as curved hooks that hinge from the knuckle. Leaving the middle finger resting on the second string, place *i* on the first string; pulling the finger from the knuckle, pluck the string and allow *i* to come to rest against the second string. As the *i* finger completes the stroke, move *m* back on the first string and repeat the whole process.

Once you have the feel, try playing the alternating *m* and *i* pattern on the second and third strings as well. Then play the alternating pattern as a series of quarter notes followed by a whole note, as shown in **Example 3**. Note that the alternation continues throughout the exercise and that the whole note in measure 2 is an *m* stroke, making the first note of measure 3 an *i* stroke. Strive for a steady rhythm and an even volume and tone.

The rest stroke, in its purest form, is used more on the classical guitar, particularly for playing single lines like melodies. The lower tension of the nylon strings make a rest stroke somewhat easier to utilize. On a steel-string guitar, a rest stroke takes a little more effort and can be difficult to integrate into fingerstyle playing. However, it is useful in some situations and an important technique to develop because it will help you grasp the concept of applying inward pressure and preloading tension on the strings, yielding a fuller tone and greater volume even when your thumb and fingers do not actually come to rest against the adjacent string.

Experiment with changing the angle at which the finger crosses the string with all three finger strokes (free, preloaded free, and rest). More angle will yield a softer tone along with less resistance. This is useful for playing fast passages. A more perpendicular angle increases resistance but yields a little louder, fuller tone. This works well for slower passages or when more volume is required. Keeping the nails filed and buffed will also make it much easier to play any of these strokes by reducing drag and friction.

Ex. 3

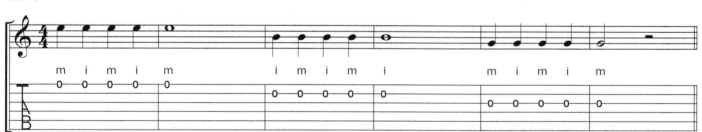

TRACK 4

The picking-hand fingers at an angle (top) and more perpendicular with the strings (bottom).

The Fretting Hand

The fingers of the fretting hand are used to press down the strings in order to fix the pitch of one or more strings at a time. As with any style of guitar playing, it's highly recommended to keep your fingernails short on the fretting hand (left hand for most players) so they don't interfere with your ability to hold down notes and chords.

The fretting-hand fingers are numbered 1–4, beginning with the index finger and ending with the pinky. The thumb of the fretting hand is used to support and guide the hand and fingers as they move around the fingerboard. The thumb should generally be centered on the back of the neck, but free enough to move both laterally and along the length of the neck to accommodate the position of the fingers. Keeping the thumb relaxed but straight will help your hand to stay relatively open—not collapsed—giving the fingers easy access to the strings, and allowing the hand to move freely up and down the fingerboard. The wrist should be kept as straight as possible, and the elbow should be relaxed and floating free from your body. (If you find this hand position difficult, it may be that you need to elevate, or get more angle on, the neck of the guitar.)

The frets are numbered in ascending order, beginning with the one closest to the headstock. Place your second finger on the fourth string at the second fret. To place a finger "at" a given fret means to place the fingertip just behind (the side closest to the nut) that fret, as shown in the photo on the next page. The fingertip should come down more or less vertical to the plane of the fingerboard, very close to but not touching the second fret. (You may notice the first finger leans toward the nut, but the fingertip should still be close to perpendicular to the fingerboard when viewed from the headstock.) With the second finger in place, position your thumb behind the neck so that it lines up with the first fret, or perhaps a bit further in the direction of the second fret. With the wrist kept straight, the thumb will likely be angled somewhat toward the headstock of the guitar.

If your wrist is twisted or bent, try pivoting your thumb from the point of contact with the back of the neck to find a position where the wrist straightens out. Hands of different sizes and shapes will require slightly different positions, and some chords and hand positions you encounter will require repositioning the thumb. As you learn to play more difficult fretting-hand positions, it will be necessary to bend the wrist at times, but whenever possible try to keep your wrist straight because this will minimize stress and fatigue on the fretting hand.

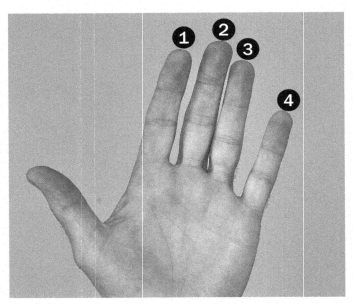

Fretting-hand fingers are identified with numerals in music notation and tab.

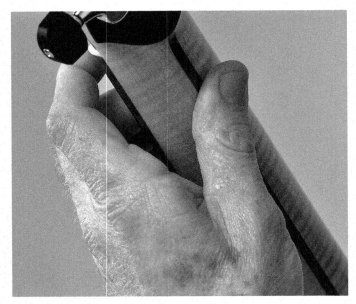

Keep the thumb relaxed and centered on the back of the guitar neck.

BASIC TECHNIQUE
The Fretting Hand

Fretting-Hand Position

With your second finger at the second fret of the fourth string, play a rest stroke with the picking-hand thumb. If there is buzzing, you will need to adjust the fretting finger to make sure it is pressing down squarely over the string just behind the fret. Without moving the fretting-hand thumb, lift the second finger about an inch above the fingerboard, and hammer it back down on to the string, taking care the fingertip stays vertical to the fingerboard. Practice this a few times, until the motion begins to feel familiar.

Now with your second finger raised slightly above the string, and without moving your fretting-hand thumb, hammer down the first finger at the first fret of the fourth string. Keeping the first finger on the string, hammer the second finger down at the second fret, keeping the fingertip perpendicular to the fingerboard. After the second finger finishes pressing the string against the fret, release the first finger from the first fret. Next, hammer the third finger down at the third fret, and then release the second finger from the second fret. Next, hammer the fourth finger down at the fourth fret, and then release the third finger from the third fret. (Because the fourth finger is significantly shorter, it will be less perpendicular to the fingerboard than the other fingers.) Repeat this process on all six strings.

You will probably notice that this exercise becomes progressively more difficult with the third and fourth fingers. The first and second fingers tend to be stronger. The third finger tends to want to move with both the second and fourth fingers, and the fourth finger (pinky) is clearly shorter and weaker than the others. With time you will build strength and flexibility in all the fingers, and especially the fourth finger.

This fretting-hand exercise was played in *first position*. In first position, the first finger of the fretting hand generally plays at the first fret, the second finger plays at the second fret, the third finger at the third fret, and the fourth finger at the fourth fret. There are, however, many exceptions to this rule. Some melodies and musical phrases will require moving fingers out of position. Many chords, especially those that have more than one note stopped at the same fret, also require placing fingers out of position. But, in general, fretting-hand position is a powerful guide for choosing which finger to use. We'll introduce other positions later on.

When fretting a note, your fingertip should be close to perpendicular with the fingerboard and just behind the fret.

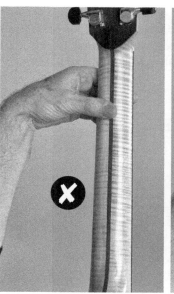 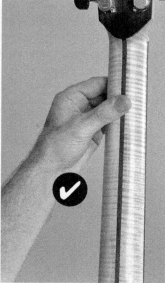

If your wrist is bent, pivot your thumb on the back of the guitar neck to find the proper playing position.

Coordination of the picking hand with the fretting hand is essential for producing cleanly played notes with a good tone. **Example 1** is a chromatic scale covering all the notes on the guitar available in first position. Practice the scale very slowly, focusing on lifting and setting down the fretting-hand fingers smoothly and evenly, and taking care not to lift the fingers before the note has sounded for its full quarter-note value and the next note is being played. To avoid any unwanted sounds, the picking-hand finger should pluck the string at the exact same time the fretting-hand finger makes contact with the string. (With time, you'll learn other techniques for moving cleanly from one note to another.) When a fretted note is followed by a note on another string, as with the G♯ at the beginning of measure 2, the finger should lift just enough to allow the string to rise off the fingerboard, but so the finger still lightly touches the string momentarily before releasing the string completely. This damps the string, preventing any unwanted sound after it's released. Experiment with playing the scale with the various strokes discussed in the picking-hand lesson: rest stroke, free stroke, and preloaded free stroke.

Both picking-hand and fretting-hand fingerings have been included in Example 1. The numbers alongside the notes indicate which fretting-hand finger is to be used. Notes without a number are played on open strings, as indicated with a 0 in the tablature. Sometimes a zero will be placed above or beside a note to be played on an open string, usually when there is no tablature. The letters for picking-hand fingerings are placed below the notes. The dashed line following the *p* beneath the very first note indicates that all the notes above it (those on the bottom three strings) should be played with the thumb. Play the notes on the top three strings using the alternating pattern of *i* and *m*.

Fingerings are not always indicated in guitar music, and when they are, they are often indicated only where the logic of fretting-hand position is not obvious or where the composer or arranger has a preference for a fingering that allows for a more successful execution of the music. It's important to pay close attention to fingerings early on, because this will help you visualize the best choice when no fingerings are provided.

Scales

Scales can be played in many different positions; most of the examples in the early part of this guide will be played in first and second position in the most commonly used keys of C, G, D, E, A and their relative minor keys (Am, Em, Bm, C♯m, and F♯m respectively). Learning to play those major scales will help get your fretting hand oriented on the fingerboard and prepare you to play the phrases in the next section. **Example 2** is a C-major scale, played in first position. Pay close attention to both fretting- and picking-hand fingerings, and practice the scale very slowly, focusing on lifting and setting down the fretting-hand fingers smoothly and evenly.

Ex. 1 Chromatic Scale

BASIC TECHNIQUE
The Fretting Hand

Ex. 2

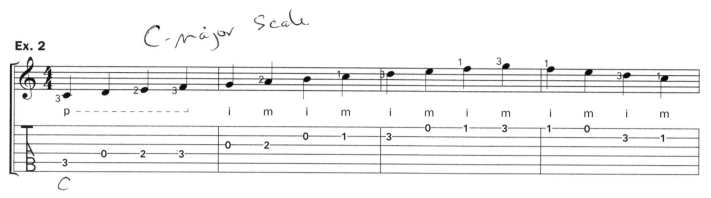

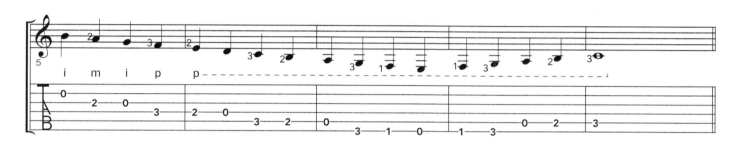

Example 3 is a G major scale played in first position. The F notes in Example 2 have changed to F♯. The F♯ is played with the fourth finger on the fourth string. This might feel like a stretch at first, but releasing the previously played E note as you are fretting the F♯ will make it easier. The F♯ on the first and sixth strings is played with the second finger. Play the scale slowly without moving the fretting-hand thumb or repositioning the fretting hand. This will provide stability and help guide the fingers to find the correct notes. Avoiding unnecessary hand movements and thinking "economy of motion" will allow you to learn more quickly. And as with all exercises, practicing slowly and in time (with a metronome!) will make your practice more consistent.

Ex. 3

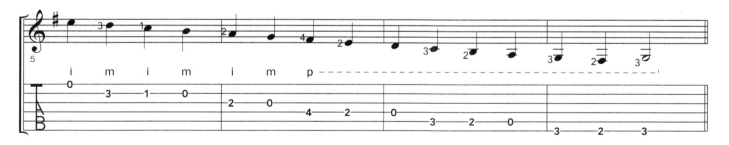

THE ALEX DE GRASSI FINGERSTYLE GUITAR METHOD   29

The D scale in **Example 4** is shown in both first and second position because phrases played in the key of D are commonly played in both positions. Playing in first position in the key of D is convenient for combining with the C and G scales above because there is no need to change the fretting-hand position. However, because no notes are played on the first fret in the key of D (the C is sharped), it is also convenient to play the scale in second position, with the first finger fretting notes at the second fret, the second finger fretting notes at the third fret, the third finger at the fourth fret, and the fourth finger at the fifth fret. Second position allows the fourth finger to reach up to play the A on the fifth fret of the first string, and many melodies in D use that note. Practice playing the D scale in both positions.

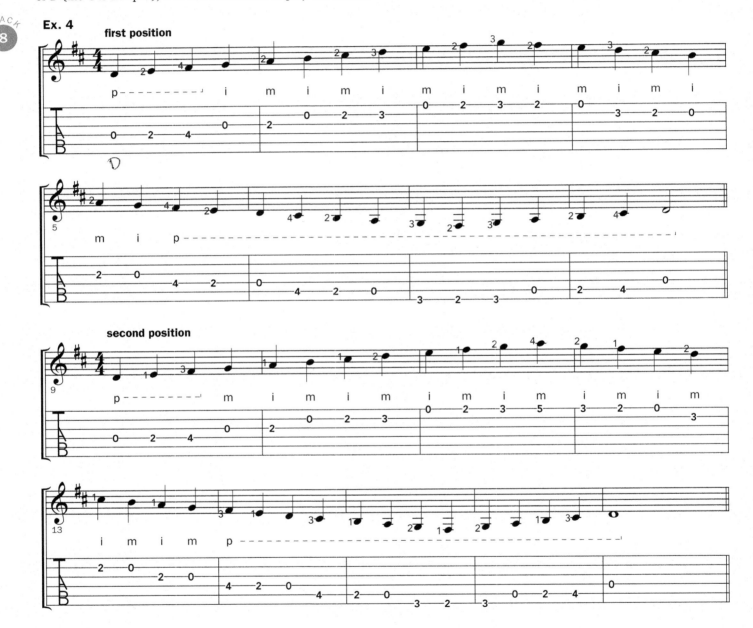

30 THE ALEX DE GRASSI FINGERSTYLE GUITAR METHOD

BASIC TECHNIQUE
The Fretting Hand

The E scale in **Example 5** is shown in first position. There are many places where the fretting-hand fingering moves between the second and fourth fingers, and the fourth and first fingers. Go slowly and remember to release the previously played note as you play the next note.

The A scale (**Example 6**) presents a new challenge. It can be played in first position, but the high A, which is often used in the key of A, can't be easily reached in first position. The scale can also be played in second position, but that makes it difficult to reach the G♯ played on the first fret of the third string. There are various solutions, one of the easiest being to change hand positions in the middle of the scale. After playing the first octave in first position, and while playing the note B on the open string, move the fretting hand up one position and continue with the second octave in second position. The open B string gives the fretting hand a short break and enough time to reposition itself before fretting the next note at the second fret of the second string with the first finger. The change from second back to first position can be made at the open string B on the way down on the downbeat of measure 6. The rest of the scale is played in first position.

As you practice these scales, remember to lift the fretting-hand fingers as you fret the next note. This is less fatiguing and allows the fingers to get ready to reposition themselves for the next notes to be played. Experiment with rest strokes and pre-loaded free strokes, and strive for an even, consistent volume and tone throughout the whole scale.

Ex. 5

Ex. 6

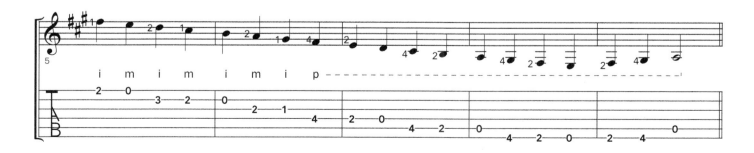

THE ALEX DE GRASSI FINGERSTYLE GUITAR METHOD 31

Section 3
First Phrases

Note Duration 34

Legato Techniques 39

Open Strings vs. Fretted Notes 46

Audio Playlist 1, Tracks 11–36

Playing a successful melody or bass line usually involves more than one string—and learning to stop strings from vibrating to define a note's value can be as important as setting them in motion. Notes can be played on open strings or as fretted notes, or connected together with a single pluck. In this section we'll look at ways to control a note's duration, the pros and cons of fretted notes vs. open string notes, and some of the legato techniques for connecting them.

Note Duration

Every note has a beginning and an end. This is called a note's *duration*, and there are two fundamental ways of controlling it. The first, releasing the note, is used with fretted notes, and the second, stopping the string with the picking hand, can be used with both open strings and with fretted notes. In theory, the value of any given note is determined by its written value: eighth note, quarter note, half note, etc. Sometimes it is desirable to let the notes ring beyond their written values, and at other times it is desirable to stop them. In practice, it can be quite complicated or simply impossible to control the precise durations of notes, especially in music with fast tempos, but with experience you will gain a greater understanding of how and when to control durations of individual notes.

Fret the fourth string at the second fret with the second fretting-hand finger and pluck the note E with the picking-hand thumb. Listen to the note gradually decay and time it. The note may last up to ten seconds or longer, depending on a variety of factors, including how hard you plucked the note and the sustaining capability of your guitar. Try it again, only this time, let it ring for a second or two. Then, lift the second finger just enough to allow the string to rise off the fingerboard, but so the finger still lightly touches the string for a moment before releasing it completely. (This makes for a clean release.) The string stops vibrating because you have controlled the note's duration by releasing the note with the fretting hand.

Now play the E an octave above on the open first string using the ring finger (*a*) of your picking hand. Let the note continue to vibrate till it can no longer be heard. Pluck the string again, let it ring for a second, then put the *a* finger back down on the string. The string stops vibrating because you have controlled the note's duration by stopping it with the picking hand. Repeat the process with the *m* and *i* fingers on the open (unfretted) second and third strings. Try to keep the thumb and other fingers resting on their respective strings as you do so. Minimizing movement of the picking-hand fingers by keeping them on or close to the strings at all times will help you develop greater control as you progress.

For now, it is enough to have a basic awareness of the durations of the notes you are playing. Play **Example 1** with the thumb and fingers on the same strings as above. Play it once, allowing the notes to ring. Play it a second time and stop each string as you pluck the next one in the sequence. The first three strings are stopped by placing the picking-hand finger back on the string, and the fourth string is stopped by releasing the string with the fretting-hand finger. (Alternatively, the fourth string can be stopped by replacing the thumb on the fourth string for the half-note rest.) Play the line several times each way, with the notes ringing and with them stopped, and listen to the difference. The first way has a fuller, more resonant sound, but the second way has more clarity. The choice will depend on the musical context.

Ex. 1

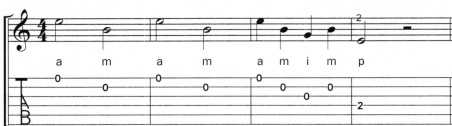

Sympathetic Vibrations

You may notice that when you stop either the E fretted on the fourth string or the E an octave higher on the open first string, the guitar still makes a sound. Try playing the E on the fourth string again, with the picking-hand fingers resting on strings one, two, and three, and after you let up with the fretting-hand finger to stop the string, cover the fifth and sixth strings with the side of your thumb and hand. The sound disappears! Those two strings were vibrating *sympathetically*. In other words, they were set in motion by the sympathetic vibration of the note you played: the sixth string vibrated because it is tuned to E, and the A string because the note E is a very strong overtone of A. If your picking-hand *a* and *m* fingers had not been covering the first and second strings (E and B), you would have also heard those strings vibrating sympathetically as well.

FIRST PHRASES
Note Duration

Now try Example 1 again and let the notes continue to sound until you reach the fourth string in measure 4. As you play the fourth string with the thumb, replace the three fingers *a*, *m*, and *i* back down on the strings. Played this way, the phrase sounds very open with all the notes connected or *legato,* but by stopping the top three strings as you play the final note, the phrase has a sense of completion because the only note continuing to ring is the last note. Alternatively, you could wait for the last note to ring for two beats and then put the thumb and fingers down together, giving the phrase a more abrupt ending.

To make a complete rest in the last two beats of the final measure, place the side of your thumb across strings four, five, and six so that it stops the lower three strings simultaneously. To do this, collapse your hand somewhat by flattening (straightening) the knuckles slightly and increasing the bend of the fingers at the second joint, while lowering the base of your thumb so that the thumb and lower part of your hand is touching the three bass strings. With your fingers remaining on the top three strings, the guitar should now be completely silent. The action of stopping the lower three strings with the thumb should be decisive, but gentle and even enough so as not to add any unwanted noise. It will be easier with the three fingers still resting on the upper strings, as they will stabilize the hand and minimize any unnecessary movement. This will take some practice, and, remember, economy of motion is the mantra that will help you learn more rapidly.

Bass Lines

Sometimes a musical line falls such that it is convenient to control the note durations just by using rest strokes. This works particularly well for stopping open strings in descending bass lines. Play **Example 2** using only the thumb to play a series of rest strokes.

As the thumb comes to rest against the adjacent string, it stops the previous note from sounding. While the first three notes are stopped by releasing the fretted note E and then refretting the E to stop the D, the D played on the open fourth string on the first beat of measure 3 is stopped by the rest stroke playing the C on the adjacent fifth string. Likewise, the open-string note A on the fourth beat of measure 3 is stopped by playing a rest stroke on the sixth string. After two beats, the thumb comes back down to stop the open sixth string and mute any resonance on strings four and five for the final half-note rest.

Play the line again using free strokes and try to avoid stopping any vibrating open strings with fretting-hand fingers so that the open fourth, fifth, and sixth strings continue to ring as you complete the example. As shown in **Example 3**, the open D string continues to sound throughout measure 3, and all three open string notes (D, A, and E) continue to ring as a chord in the final measure. Compare that sound with the example using rest strokes.

There might be situations where it is desirable to let one or more of those bass notes ring, but generally speaking, allowing

Picking-hand thumb and fingers stopping all six strings.

Ex. 2 — TRACK 12

Ex. 3 — TRACK 13

too many low notes to ring beyond their written values makes the music sound muddy, especially where there are changes in the chords or the harmony.

Many ascending lines do not require any string stopping because any open-string notes are stopped by fretting the successive note on that string. In **Example 4**, the first note E is stopped by playing the following fretted note, F♯, on the same string. Likewise, the open-string A at the end of measure 1 and the open string D in measure 2 are stopped by simply fretting the following notes B and E, respectively. These note durations are automatically controlled, and they can be played using either rest or preloaded free strokes.

But some ascending lines require string stopping. In **Example 5a**, after you play the second note A on the downbeat of the first full measure, the thumb must quickly return to the sixth string long enough to stop the pickup note E before moving on to play the B note on the fifth string. Likewise, after playing the note E on the downbeat of measure 3, the thumb must quickly return to the fifth string to stop the note A from continuing to sound on the open fifth string.

This kind of string stopping can be done at slow tempos or with long notes, but becomes nearly impossible at faster tempos or where shorter notes are being played. An alternative solution is to refinger the A note, as shown in **Example 5b**, so that it is played as a fretted note on the sixth string, thus eliminating the need for picking-hand string stopping. Note that the new fingering shifts the fretting hand to *second position*, requiring that the other fretted notes be refingered as well. In second position, the fretting-hand fingers are typically assigned so that fretting-hand fingers one through four play on frets two through five, respectively.

With this revised fingering, you can control the note durations by simply releasing the fretted notes as you play successive notes. The extra effort required to make the stretch between the fifth and second frets in measure 1 is eased by the fact that the first finger does not need to come down till just before the note B is played, and by the fact that the fourth finger can be released as the B is plucked. Developing this awareness that fretting-hand fingers do not need to be in place until just before the note is to be played, and that they can be lifted after the note is completed, will save energy and reduce fatigue and stress on your fretting hand.

In practice, many bass lines have a combination of ascending and descending sequences of notes, which requires a combina-

Ex. 4

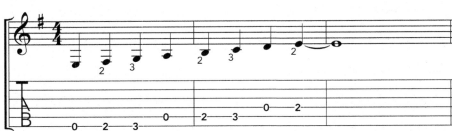

Ex. 5a

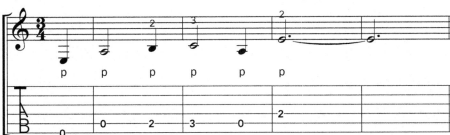

Ex. 5b

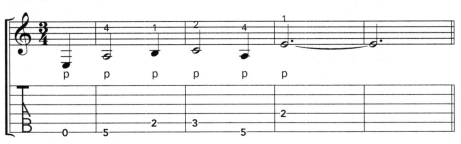

FIRST PHRASES
Note Duration

tion of the techniques we have learned so far in order to control note durations. In **Example 6**, you can control all of the fretted note durations by simply releasing the fretting-hand finger. The open strings will require some extra care. The open-string notes D in measures 1, 2, and 7, and the A on the fifth string in measure 3, can all be stopped by playing the following note with a rest stroke. The E on the open sixth string in the second half of measure 3 requires the same stopping action used in Example 5a—after playing the dotted-half-note A at the beginning of measure 4, move your thumb back to the sixth string to stop it from sounding. Then, after a count of three beats, move your thumb back to the fifth string to play the note B on the fourth beat. In practice, once you've stopped the open sixth string from vibrating, you can let your thumb off the string and wait for the fourth beat, but it is typically more relaxing to leave it on the string until just before you are ready to play the next note.

Alternatively, the whole example can be played in second position using the fourth finger to fret the A notes. In this scenario, the notes B and C are played with the first and second fretting-hand fingers respectively. Try playing the example both ways and remember to keep the picking-hand fingers *i*, *m*, *a* on strings three, two, and one throughout. At the rest on beat four of measure 8, drop the thumb and collapse the hand to cover the three low strings to silence any extra resonance.

Melody Lines

It's good practice to alternate the fingers of the picking hand when playing a sequence of notes. This allows the fingers to rest between notes, and produces a more even sound and a smoother rhythm. Sometimes sequential notes will be on the same string, and other times they will fall on different strings. When the intervals between notes are small, many of the notes will be played on one or two strings, and it is convenient to alternate with using *i* and *m*.

Play the melody in **Example 7** using alternating *i* and *m* rest strokes. The first three notes are played on the second string. The fourth note of the measure is played on the open first string, and the *i* finger has to "cross" the *m* finger in order to play the note E. This may feel a little awkward at first, but with time it will feel natural.

You can control the durations of many notes in the example by simply lifting the fretting-hand finger as you play the next note. Some notes on open strings are automatically controlled by fretting the following note on the same string, as is the case with

The *i* finger "crosses" the *m* finger to play the first string in Example 7.

Ex. 6

Ex. 7

the E notes on the fourth beat of measure 1 and the third beat of measure 5.

The third note (E) in the second measure played on the open first string will continue to sound beyond its value unless it is stopped. You could stop it with your picking-hand *a* finger, but it might be easier to damp it with the third fretting-hand finger by slightly flattening, or changing the angle of the finger as you place it to play the following note D. The finger thus stops the open first string as you fret the second string. This fretting-hand *string damping* technique, yet another way to control note durations, can also be used to stop the open-string note E on the first beat of measures 5 and 7.

For some melodies, it is preferable to use the *a* finger in addition to the *i* and *m* fingers, especially when the melody plays across the strings, as in **Example 8**. This is typical of melodies with larger intervals between notes, and also becomes useful as melodies are integrated into polyphonic arrangements that have bass lines and, perhaps, other parts.

When you use all three fingers—*a*, *m*, and *i*—it can become awkward to play a rest stroke. So, try playing the passage using preloaded free strokes. As in Example 7, most of the note durations in the line can be controlled by releasing or fretting a note. To stop the open-string notes, replace the picking-hand finger that plucked the note back down on the same string. For instance, when playing the second note (C) in measure 1, place the *a* finger back down on the first string to stop the first note (E) from sounding. This happens again in measures 3 and 5. Alternatively, you might stop the strings with the fretting-hand string-damping tech-

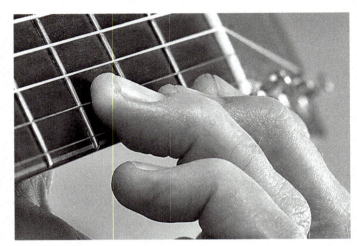

Flattening your fretting finger to damp adjacent strings is an effective way to control note durations.

nique introduced in Example 7. You will need to replace the picking-hand *i* finger to stop the G on the open third string in measures 4 and 6.

Even if you have successfully stopped all the strings as described above, you may have noticed some background resonance. This is the sound of the overtones generated by the lower three strings vibrating sympathetically. Most of that sound is coming from the open fifth string (A) because the melody centers around the pitch A. Play the passage again with the thumb resting on the fifth string, and most of that resonance will disappear.

Ex. 8

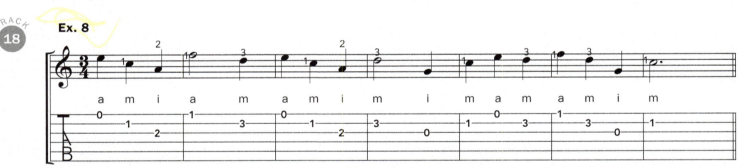

FIRST PHRASES
Legato Techniques

Legato Techniques

Sometimes it is desirable to connect two or more notes of different pitches by plucking a string only once. This is possible using a technique traditionally called *legato*, from the Italian word *legare*, meaning to join or tie together. In fingerstyle playing, the three fundamental legato techniques are known as the *hammer-on, pull-off,* and *slide*. These can be used to create a more fluid, connected phrasing of a musical line, and to vary the texture in the music. Hammer-ons, pull-offs, and slides can also facilitate execution of musical passages requiring speed.

Hammer-ons and pull-offs are graphically represented by a slur, or curved line, connecting the notes, as shown in **Example 1**. When the pitch ascends, the slur represents a hammer-on. When the pitch descends, the slur represents a pull-off. The tablature might be additionally marked with an *H* for a hammer-on, and a *P* for a pull-off, though this marking is not considered necessary.

Hammer-Ons

A hammer-on can begin with plucking either an open or a fretted note. Each hammer-on in **Example 2** begins with an eighth note played on an open string followed by a hammered eighth note (note that this example is played in second position). In preparation, the fretting-hand finger should be raised as much as an inch above the fingerboard. After you pluck the open string with the designated picking-hand finger, hammer the fretting-hand finger down quickly, keeping the fingertip perpendicular to the fingerboard. The motion should originate by engaging the knuckle joint of the fretting-hand finger, utilizing the same "hinge" mechanism previously described for the picking-hand fingers.

The hammer-on motion should be smooth but forceful, with the fretting-hand finger coming to rest just behind the fret. The string is pinned against the fret, causing the note to sound. Play Example 2 very slowly at first, taking care to keep the tempo steady so that the notes have equal durations. The volume of the hammered note will be determined by a combination of how hard the string is plucked and how fast the finger is hammered down. Experiment with these two variables to balance the volume of the plucked note with the hammered note. Though the note durations of hammered notes can be controlled by releasing the fretting-hand finger, try also replacing the picking-hand fingers to stop the hammered notes as you pluck the successive strings; that may clean up the overall sound by eliminating unwanted resonance resulting from lifting fretting-hand fingers off the strings.

Hammer-ons that begin by plucking a fretted note have the advantage that a fretting-hand finger is already in position on the fingerboard, thus helping to stabilize the hand and guiding the hammering finger into position. However, this movement also

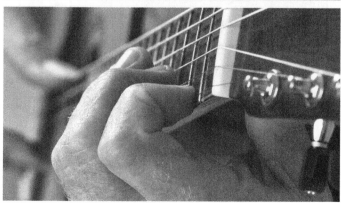

Raise the finger as much as an inch off the fingerboard before playing a hammer-on.

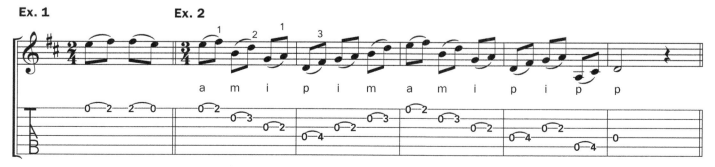

requires a little more concentration to move the fretting-hand fingers independently from one another. In particular, the second note (G) in **Example 3** requires some extra strength and coordination for the relatively weak fourth finger (the pinky) to hammer on the fifth fret while holding down the F♯ on the fourth fret with the third finger. The remaining hammer-ons in the exercise will probably be easier, but will also take some care to control the fingers independently.

After playing Example 3, you may hear some unwanted resonance from the guitar. Most likely this will be the open sixth and, to a lesser degree, the open fifth string vibrating sympathetically with the notes E and A played in the next-to-last measure (these notes are an octave above the open strings). You can stop this resonance by placing the side of the thumb down on those two strings after playing the final note D of the exercise. Alternatively, you could play the final note D by fretting the fifth string at the fifth fret with the fourth finger, thereby stopping the open A string. The picking-hand thumb would still need to stop resonance from the vibrating sixth string. As with Example 2, replacing picking-hand fingers on the previously played string as you pluck the next one will also clean up the sound.

Pull-Offs

Pull-offs always begin by plucking a fretted note and then pulling the fretting-hand finger off the string to sound either another fretted note or an open string, as shown in **Example 4**. It is generally easier to pull off the first string, because the fretting-hand fingers are less impeded by the other strings, so it's a good idea to practice the technique on the first string before moving to the others.

The pull-off movement is similar to the plucking action used by the picking-hand fingers. After plucking the fretted note with the designated picking-hand finger, the fretting-hand finger pulls the string toward the edge of the fingerboard slightly, and plucks it firmly to release. The fretting hand does not need to move much, but the fretting-hand finger used for the pull-off will recoil by pulling back from the knuckle joint. The tip of the finger may curl somewhat, but engaging the knuckle joint will ultimately give you more power and control.

Exerting a little extra downward pressure (against the fingerboard) on the string with the fretting-hand finger in preparation for the pull-off will give a little more snap to the string as you release it. This, in combination with a decisive plucking action of the fretting-hand finger, will yield a crisper sound. As with ham-

Ex. 3

Ex. 4

Ex. 5

FIRST PHRASES
Legato Techniques

mer-ons, you can control the volume of the pull-off by adjusting how forcefully the picking hand initially plucks the string, and how forcefully the fretting-hand finger pulls off the string. Experiment with these two variables to try to get a balanced volume between the plucked and pulled-off notes.

Executing pull-offs cleanly on the other strings, as shown in **Example 5,** can be more challenging. As the fretting-hand finger pulls and releases, it is likely to either come to rest on the adjacent string, or to touch the adjacent string as it continues to move away from the fingerboard. Using picking-hand string-stopping technique to damp the adjacent strings prevents them from sounding inadvertently. For example, as you pluck the second string with the *m* finger, replace the *a* finger on the first string; as you pluck the third string with the *i* finger, replace the *m* finger on the second string; and so on. After holding the last note for three beats, place the side of the picking-hand thumb across strings 6, 5, and 4 for a clean finish. As with the first string, exerting a little extra downward pressure on the other strings in preparation for the pull-off will help to achieve a crisp sound.

The finger executing the pull-off must avoid touching the adjacent string altogether when that string is sounding a note. This can be achieved by landing the finger on the string more toward the pad side of the tip (away from the nail) at an angle slightly beyond perpendicular. This allows the fingertip to reach under the string slightly, then pull *up* and away from the fingerboard with some snap, avoiding touching the adjacent string. Practice this "reaching under" technique for the pull-offs in **Example 6** to allow the open strings to ring through. A "push-off" (reverse pull-off) is sometimes useful for avoiding the adjacent strings when playing on the sixth string. After fretting the note, the finger pushes the string toward the edge of the bass side of the fingerboard by straightening the fingertip joint and lifting

The fretting-hand position before and after a pull-off.

up and away from the string. Try this on the pull-off from G to E on beat two of the third measure. Remember to strive for a balanced volume and tone as you practice Examples 5 and 6.

Combining Slurs

Hammer-ons and pull-offs are often used together to play phrases. As with hammer-ons, pulling off with the weaker fourth finger is a challenge, so it's good to give more attention to the pinky as you practice these techniques. **Example 7** uses the fourth finger in combination with other fretting-hand fingers wherever possible. Practice the reaching-under and push-off techniques to allow the open fourth and fifth strings to ring in measures 2 and 3. Use picking-hand string stopping to avoid triggering unwanted notes.

Double or even triple hammer-ons and pull-offs are played by holding the first hammered or pulled note, then hammering on or pulling off of the successive notes. In **Example 8** it's important to add a little extra force to the hammer-ons and pull-offs occurring at the beginning of each measure to emphasize the downbeat. Note the triple pull-off beginning on the last two notes of measure 4 and continuing on the first two notes of measure 5. Be sure to add a little extra force to the second of those three pull-offs to emphasize the F♯ on the downbeat. Again, using picking-hand string stopping as you move from string to string will reduce unwanted notes and noises produced by fingers pulling off and touching adjacent strings. For example, as the first finger pulls off from the C♯ to sound the open B string on the downbeat of measure 2, it may touch the open first string. If the *a* finger is resting on the first string, that unwanted note will not sound.

You can also tie together hammer-ons and pull-offs so that a pull-off is directly followed by a hammer-on (or vice versa) without replucking the note. Many of the eighth-note triplets in **Example 9** are tied together in that manner to give a more fluid feel to the 6/8 rhythm typical of Celtic music.

After plucking the first note E, hold the note for the first triplet. Then the second finger pulls off to sound the second triplet, and without plucking the string again, the second finger comes back down to sound the third triplet. The sequence is reversed beginning on the last eighth note (B) of the second group of triplets—this time a hammer-on to the downbeat (C) of the third group of triplets is followed by a pull-off to the second triplet (B) in that group.

Work through the exercise slowly. Counting each measure 1 2 3, 2 2 3 will help you feel the rhythm and keep track of where you are. Try to give each note the same duration and volume, and give the downbeat of each triplet a little emphasis, even if the note is hammered or pulled. Note that in measures 3–4, there are four notes tied together with one pluck of the string. The last triplet of the second beat in measure 3 is followed by a hammer-on, a pull-off, and another hammer-on for a combined triple hammer-on/pull-off!

Ex. 8

Ex. 9

FIRST PHRASES
Legato Techniques

Slides

Another legato technique for connecting two notes together with a single picking-hand stroke is the *slide*. The slide is graphically represented by a straight line between two notes (in addition to the slur marking), and it is used to connect two *fretted* notes—very often notes that are a half or whole tone (one or two frets) away from each other—by sliding a single fretting-hand finger along the string from one fret to another. The slide (sometimes referred to as *glissando*) has a fluid quality, de-emphasizing the attack of the note the finger slides to, making it perhaps even more legato than hammer-ons and pull-offs.

Play the first five notes of **Example 10** and apply a little extra pressure toward the fingerboard with the third fretting-hand finger as it slides over the second fret to change the pitch on the first two notes from B to C, and again on the fourth and fifth notes to change the pitch from E to F. This will produce more volume and a more defined sound. Because a single fretting-hand finger is used to slide from one fret to another, the choice of finger will affect the position of the fretting hand after the slide. Using the third finger to start both of these slides allows the fretting hand to stay in first position. This requires only minimal movement of the fretting hand, and the thumb can remain in a fixed position behind the neck.

Half-step slides, spanning a single fret, do not usually require changing the fretting-hand position. However, slides spanning two frets or more generally do require a position change. Using the fourth finger on beat one-*and* (if you're counting one-and two-and three-and four-and) of the second measure to slide up two frets, from D to E, requires simultaneously sliding the fretting-hand thumb along the back of the neck to allow the hand to move into second position. Try it a few times and check the position of your fretting-hand thumb before and after the slide.

With the fretting hand now in second position, the first finger can easily reach the following note G on the third fret of the first string, slide it down one fret to the F♯, and then play the next three notes (D, A, F♯)—all without leaving second position. The next three notes are played on open strings, giving the fretting hand more than enough time to return to first position so the third finger can easily slide from the second to the third fret to end the phrase on the low G. This demonstrates a very important principle: notes played on open strings free up the fretting hand, giving it time to move to a new position.

Slides can be combined with hammer-ons and pull-offs to vary the legato quality of a phrase, as in **Example 11**. Using rest strokes will control the duration of the second D on the open fourth string in measure 1 and also keep that string from sounding as you pull off from the B to the A on the adjacent fifth string on the downbeat of measure 2.

Ex. 10

Ex. 11

Playing Melodies with Slurs

Example 12 ("Oh! Susannah") and **Example 13** ("Celtic Melody") mix hammer-ons, pull-offs, and slides with individually plucked notes. Pay close attention to note durations and use the picking-hand and fretting-hand string-stopping techniques presented earlier as well as the thumb rest stroke wherever it seems appropriate. After you've learned to play these songs, experiment with note durations and allow some notes to ring as you play successive notes. Also, experiment with playing some of the legato notes as individual, plucked notes, and try connecting some of the individually plucked notes with hammer-ons, pull-offs, and slides. Listen to how the presence or absence of these legato techniques can affect the nature of the phrase.

Ex. 12: "Oh! Susannah"

FIRST PHRASES
Legato Techniques

Ex. 13: "Celtic Melody"

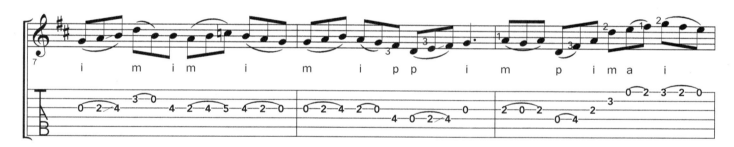

THE ALEX DE GRASSI FINGERSTYLE GUITAR METHOD

Open Strings vs. Fretted Notes

On the guitar the same pitch can often be played on several strings in different positions on the neck. In standard tuning, the open string notes are E1, A1, D2, G2, B2, and E3 (the numbers indicate the octave; E3, for instance, is two octaves above E1). For those notes, you will often have a choice of playing either the fretted note or the open string note. Look at **Example 1** and play each of the open strings and then the equivalent pitch as a fretted note found on the lower adjacent string (these are the same pairings you use to tune your strings). Logically enough, there is no fretted equivalent for the open sixth string.

The decision to use an open string or a fretted note might be based on a variety of considerations. One of those might simply be convenience. Is it easy to play? Another consideration is controlling note durations. Should each note end before the next begins, or should they be allowed to overlap? We've already seen how it's possible to control notes with the picking hand and the fretting hand, so let's look how these two considerations affect the choice of an open vs. a fretted note in a musical phrase.

Many of the notes in **Example 2** are played open for convenience; it is less work for the fretting hand, and the notes fall comfortably under the picking hand. Play through the example allowing the open strings to ring, and you'll hear it has a pleasing sound. However, if the nature of the music suggested that we maintain strict quarter-note durations, it would be necessary to stop the open strings with the picking-hand fingers. Play the exercise again very slowly, releasing fretted notes after their written values, and stopping the open strings with the finger that plucked them as you pluck the succeeding note. This makes the passage considerably more challenging.

As an alternative way of controlling the note durations, in **Example 3** the open-string notes have been replaced by fretted notes, and the passage is now played in second position. This eliminates the need for stopping any strings with the picking hand, and makes it easier to maintain strict quarter note durations simply by releasing the fretting-hand finger as you play the succeeding note. It is a more "discreet" way of playing the line. However, it is more work for the fretting hand.

In particular, the first two notes of measure 2 are played on adjacent strings two and three using the same finger (the fourth) for both notes. In order to do this, it is necessary to straighten the fourth finger in preparation for playing those two notes while the second finger frets the D on the last beat of measure 1. The fourth

A Note on Fingering

In Example 2, the G at the downbeat of measure 6 is played at the third fret with the fourth finger. This fingering does not change the fretting-hand position, but rather contracts the range of the position, making the fingering easier for two reasons: 1) the third finger has just fretted a note on the second string and would have to move very quickly in order to fret the first string; and 2) it eases the stretch for the first finger to reach the following note C fretted at the first fret of the second string.

Ex. 1

Ex. 2

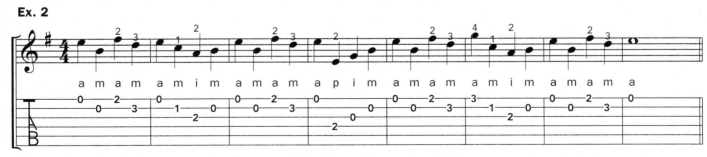

FIRST PHRASES
Open Strings vs. Fretted Notes

finger is then placed at the fifth fret, parallel to the fingerboard, such that the fingertip joint is covering both the second and third strings, with the tip of the finger extending slightly beyond the third string. Pluck the second string, and as its duration comes to an end, bend the last joint of the fourth finger just enough to lift up on the second string to stop it from vibrating, keeping the fingertip pressed down on the third string as you pluck it. (Alternatively, the fourth finger could fret the first two notes of measure 2 by lifting it off the first note and moving it over to the second note on the third string. This can be done at slow tempos but is quite difficult for medium and fast tempo passages.)

Musical Intention

While tablature is very useful (and essential for altered tunings) for understanding where notes are played on the guitar, standard notation usually offers more information about the intent of the music. Most fingerstyle guitar arrangements are *polyphonic*, meaning that they consist of separate lines such as a melody, a bass line, and perhaps a third line in the form of a countermelody, harmony, or rhythmic pattern. These individual lines are called *voices*, and they function like the voices in a choir singing different parts such as soprano, alto, tenor, baritone, etc. Some tablature systems (most notably that developed by fingerstyle guitar authority John Stropes) contain considerable detail about note durations, but standard notation can tell the player more about these individual voices in the arrangement and how they are phrased by the way the notes the notes are grouped. Whether the intent is a single voice or polyphony, the choice of fingering can help define not only note durations, but which notes belong to which voice. Often that fingering choice is between a fretted note and a note played on an open string.

Example 4 has exactly the same sequence of notes as Examples 2 and 3, but it has been rewritten to change the intention of the music. Two things have been changed: some of the individual note durations have been lengthened, and the sequence has been split into two separate voices. There is now an upper voice (melody) with stems up, and a lower voice (countermelody) with stems down.

Ex. 3

Ex. 4

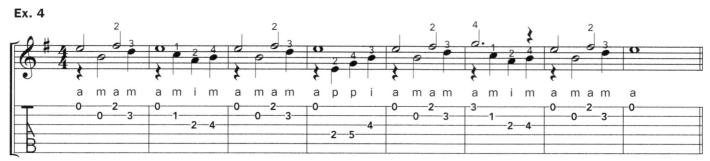

Notice that many of the open strings have been restored, as in Example 2. However, some notes that could be played open, such as the pitch B in measures 2, 4, and 6, are played as fretted notes. The new fingering has been arranged to facilitate the intention of the music so that there is almost no need to stop strings with the picking hand, and so it is relatively easy to hold and release the fretted notes to obtain the correct note durations. As you play through the example, try to hear the two voices as separate parts. Play the notes in the upper voice loudly and the notes of the lower voice softly.

Example 5 was written for two voices, or parts. Even though only a single note is plucked on each quarter-note beat, the directions of the stems, the note durations, and how the notes are grouped clearly indicate two separate voices. Both fretting-hand and picking-hand fingerings, as well as the choice of open string vs. fretted note, reflect all three considerations discussed above: controlling the note duration and best expressing the musical intent, while also trying to make the passage as convenient as possible to play. Some of the open-string notes in the upper voice can be stopped with the picking hand, and the lower-voice G tied over from measure 8 to 9 can be stopped by playing a rest stroke with *p* on the F♯ that follows. Note that *p* is used to play many of the second-voice notes on the third string. Using the thumb in opposition to the fretting-hand fingers also helps delineate the two voices.

As with most guitar music, there may be some alternate fingerings that could work as well. For example, the G notes in the lower voice in measures 4, 6, and 14 could be played on the open string. That might make it somewhat easier for the fretting hand, but it makes it more difficult to control note durations with the picking hand. Like many things in life, making good fingering choices involves some trade-offs.

Ex. 5

Section 4
Chords and Arpeggios

Strummed, Block, and Rolled Chords..... 50

Chord Voicings 54

Arpeggios 59

Audio Playlist 1, Tracks 37–57

A chord is typically defined as three or more notes played simultaneously. Most common chords include the intervals of the tonic, the third (major or minor), and the fifth (perfect, diminished, or augmented). These three intervals played together are called a *triad*. A chord can also have only two notes, but without these three intervals, the chord is hard to name, because it could be one of many chords.

In this section we'll work with chords that are commonly found in guitar music, and then we will discuss chord voicings and arpeggios. Because understanding the relationship of pitches is so central to the following discussion of chords, some of the exercises in this section will use only standard musical notation and not include tablature.

Strummed, Block, and Rolled Chords

There are many ways to play chords using fingerstyle techniques. In this lesson we will cover strummed, block, and rolled chords. Fretting-hand fingerings will be designated where deemed necessary.

Strummed Chords

Let's begin with strummed chords. Play the Em chord in **Example 1** by placing the third fretting finger on the fourth string at the second fret, taking care not to damp any of the other strings. Place the picking-hand thumb on the fourth string and sweep it across strings 4, 3, 2, and 1 in one smooth motion. The direction of the arrow to the left of the chord indicates a strum from the lowest note to the highest note—often referred to as a *down-strum*. (In this case *down* refers to the physical direction of the strum—the direction of the arrow refers to the direction of the pitches). Keep the thumb straight, and move it from the joint where it meets the hand using the lever action described in "The Picking Hand" and shown in the photos below. This will minimize movement of the hand, allowing it to remain closer to the strings and in position to resume plucking individual notes. Once again, economy of motion!

Strum the Em chord a few times and vary the speed at which the thumb moves across the strings. When strummed quickly, the notes of the chord are heard more or less simultaneously—as indicated by a straight arrow. However, when strummed slowly, the chord sounds like a series of notes played in rapid succession—as indicated by a squiggly arrow to the left of the chord in measure 2. The last note (highest pitch) of the series is typically sounded on the downbeat. This is illustrated in measure 3, where the first three notes of the chord are represented as *grace notes* that precede the downbeat. Theoretically, grace notes have no time value of their own—they either sound just prior to the note or chord, or they steal time from the note or chord they precede by beginning right on the downbeat. (See the Texture section for more on grace notes.) In this case, the three grace notes sound just prior to the chord, and the last note of the chord sounds precisely on the downbeat. All four notes continue to sound as part of the chord for the full four beats of the whole note. Very slow strums are sometimes written as a series of very short notes preceding the downbeat of the chord, as shown in measures 4 and 5.

Two notes are added to the chord in measure 6 to make a six-note Em chord. With the third fretting-hand finger still in position, place the second fretting-hand finger on the fifth string at the second fret. Beginning with the sixth string, strum across all six strings rapidly with the picking-hand thumb as indicated by the straight arrow. Then play the same chord using a slow strum, as indicated in measure 7 by the squiggly arrow and as indicated in measure 8 by the use of grace notes. Try it again, beginning the slow strum on the downbeat so the last note sounds an eighth note after the downbeat. Played this way, the five grace notes occupy the space of the first eighth note of the measure, as notated in measure 9. Continue to practice Example 1 using a metronome and tapping your foot, and focus on where the notes of the chord sound in relationship to the beat.

Strums can also play notes from highest to lowest—a so-called *up-strum*. This is indicated by an arrow pointing down as

When playing a down-strum, the thumb moves downward and remains straight.

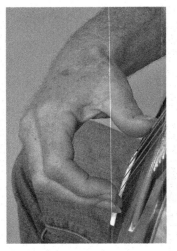 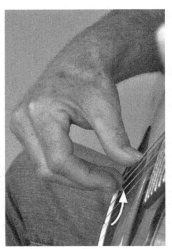

When playing an up-strum, the strumming finger maintains an arc and moves from the knuckle.

CHORDS AND ARPEGGIOS
Strummed, Block, and Rolled Chords

shown for the G chord in measure 1 of **Example 2**. For a single up-strum, any finger can be used—try them all. The strumming finger should maintain some arc for strength and hinge at the knuckle as it pulls across the strings, minimizing the movement of the hand. The strumming finger can be supported by squeezing the fingers together and moving them as one. Though the *a* finger is weaker, it is the least likely to crash into the thumb and pull the picking hand out of position. This is helpful when the up-strum is followed immediately by notes to be individually plucked by the thumb, as in measures 2–4. Note that the up-strums do not play the bass notes that were plucked at the beginning of the measure.

For continuous strumming, both down-strums and up-strums are used. This is more easily accomplished by using the thumb for both. To play the up-strums, the thumb moves with a reverse-lever action, with the back of the nail and side of the thumb brushing across the strings. The down-strums typically play on the beat, and the up-strums play the offbeats as shown in **Example 3**. Note that the arrows are all straight, indicating rapid strums that sound the notes of the chords more or less simultaneously. Using the lever and reverse-lever action will minimize hand movement. That allows for greater control and quick repositioning of thumb and fingers to pluck individual notes. An

THE ALEX DE GRASSI FINGERSTYLE GUITAR METHOD 51

individually plucked note is combined with up and down strumming in measure 4.

Individual strums are often used to accentuate a particular chord, often at the beginning or end of a phrase. Continuous strumming is a good way to play a rhythm guitar part to accompany a singer or other instrumentalists.

Block Chords

Guitarists often use the term *block chords* for chords in which the individual notes are plucked simultaneously with the thumb and fingers. The sound is different, perhaps a bit cleaner or more defined than strummed chords. Block chords limit the player to four- or possibly five-note chords (since that is how many fingers are available); however, they do offer the advantage of making it easier to select which strings to play.

The first chord in **Example 4** is a Em triad played on strings 4, 3, and 2 with picking-hand fingers *p, i,* and *m*. Like most block chords, the Em is played using free strokes for both the thumb and fingers. In measure 2 a fourth note is also played with the *a* finger on the first string, doubling the pitch of the root (E) of the chord with the E an octave above. In measure 3 only three notes of the Em triad are played (using *p, i, m*) but the root is now played an octave down. (Note that it is difficult to strum this chord without playing both the fourth and fifth strings as well; you will need to damp them both.) In measure 4, the tonic is doubled again by adding the E two octaves above to create a four-note chord played with *p, i, m, a*.

In preparation for playing block chords, place your thumb and fingers on the strings according to the placement discussed in "The Picking Hand." As you play the chord, the thumb should move in the opposite direction from the fingers, with equal pressure applied to all strings. This will produce a balanced volume and even tone across the strings and also minimize movement of the hand, leaving it in a position just above the strings, ready to play the next chord. The picking-hand fingers should be lightly touching each other and move as a single unit. Remember to *pull* the fingers from the knuckle joint as if the joint were a hinge and the fingers a closing door.

Strive to play all the notes of the chord simultaneously, so that they are heard as a block. After the chord sounds for its full half-note value, return the fingers to the strings as a single unit, firmly but gently. The next chord is played without hesitation. In measures 5–8, the same chords appear as quarter notes with quarter-note rests in between. After playing the chord and waiting a beat, the hand returns to the strings to stop them, then waits for a beat before plucking the chord again. To silence all resonance during the rests, collapse the picking hand and drop the thumb across strings 4–6 while returning the fingers to strings 1–3 (see "Note Duration" for review). Practice with a metronome to get a nice rhythmic flow of chord, rest, chord, etc.

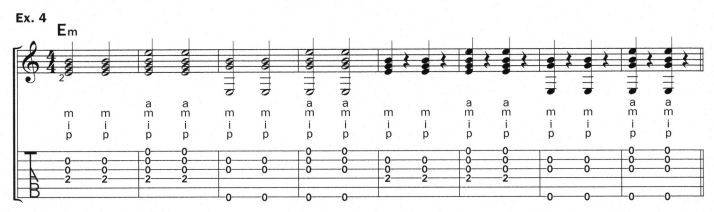

CHORDS AND ARPEGGIOS
Strummed, Block, and Rolled Chords

Rolled Chords

Rolled chords sound similar to strummed chords, and they are indicated in the music using the same squiggly arrow to the left of the chord. But like block chords, they are played with a combination of thumb and fingers, making it easy to select which strings to play. The thumb and fingers are placed on the strings, and the notes are played in rapid succession by "rolling" the fingers in the order *p–i–m–a*. It should feel like a ripple passing from your thumb and fingers. Before rolling the chords in **Example 5**, play them first as block chords, then play the individual notes slowly in sequence from bottom to top. Then roll them.

Rolled chords spread out the attack a bit, bringing a little extra attention to the individual notes. They are often used for emphasis at the beginning or end of a phrase, though they can be used anywhere. Like strummed chords, they can be rolled rapidly (to sound nearly like a block chord) or very slowly to sound like a series of grace notes preceding the final note of the chord. Experiment rolling the notes at different speeds with the last note landing on the downbeat.

It's possible to extend the number of notes in a rolled chord by playing more than one string with the thumb. This combines the strumming technique with the rolled chord technique. Play the C and Am chords in **Example 6** by first placing *p* on the fifth string and *i, m, a* on strings 3, 2, and 1, respectively. Strum the first two notes (C and E) on the adjacent fifth and fourth string with *p* a few times while leaving the picking-hand fingers in place. Once you have the feel, strum the two lowest strings again and continue to play the top three strings by rolling the fingers. Try to play the extended rolled chord with the same continuous, fluid motion used for four-note chords. To play all six notes of the G and E chords, place *p* on the sixth string and *i, m, a* on strings 3, 2, and 1, respectively. This time the thumb will strum across three strings (6, 5, and 4). Once you've got the feel of strumming the three lower strings fluidly with *i, m, a* resting on the top three strings, strum the lower three strings and continue to roll the top three strings with the fingers. Practice getting all the notes to sound evenly and at the same volume.

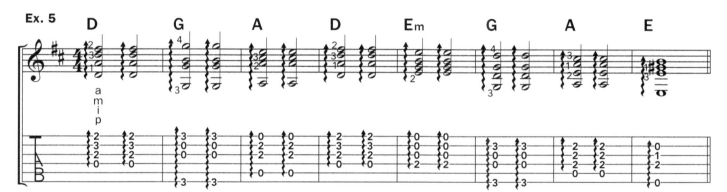

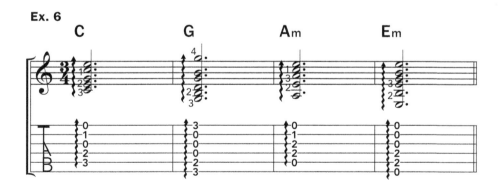

Chord Voicings

The individual notes of a chord are often referred to as *voices*. Like the different voices (soprano, alto, tenor, and bass) singing different pitches in a choir, each note in the chord represents an interval of that chord. A *chord voicing* refers to how those intervals are combined. In any given situation, there are often many chord voicing options—making a good choice will depend on a variety of factors.

Example 1 shows a variety of voicings for common chords played in first position. Strum, or roll, the C chord in measure 1. The chord you just played contains the notes C3, E3, G3, C4, and E4 (as explained earlier, the number represents the octave; for instance, C4, middle C, is an octave higher than C3). C3 is the tonic, or root; E3 is the major third; and the G3 is the perfect fifth. The pitches C4 and E4 represent the octave and the tenth (the tenth is the same pitch as the third an octave higher). Those last two notes do fatten up the sound of the chord, but it is not necessary or always desirable to duplicate pitches. The chord can be revoiced to eliminate one or more of those duplicated pitches.

In the second measure of Example 1 a simple C triad is played as a block chord with the *p, i,* and *a* fingers. This voicing is useful in some circumstances, but sounds a bit low without a context. In measure 3, the octave C is added to achieve a fuller sound that also reinforces the tonic. This chord, like all of the four-note chords in the example, is played with *p, i, m, a*. In measure 4, the E on the fourth string is omitted and replaced by the E on the open first string. This voicing has a more open sound,

Ex. 1

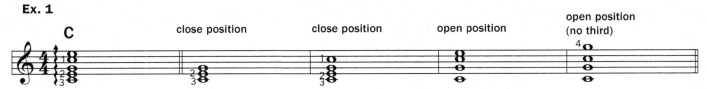

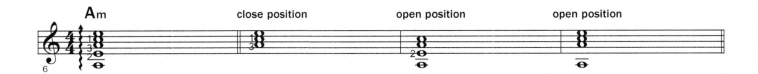

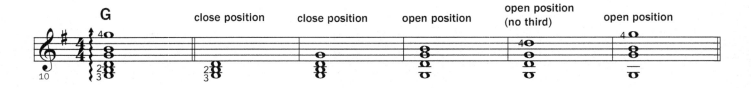

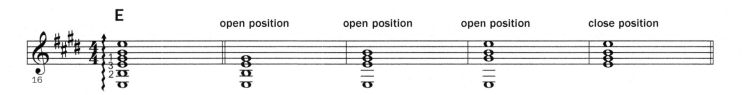

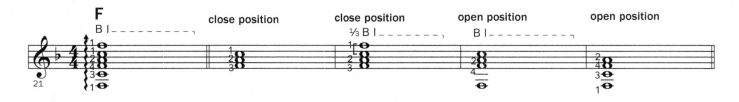

54   THE ALEX DE GRASSI FINGERSTYLE GUITAR METHOD

CHORDS AND ARPEGGIOS
Chord Voicings

and is considered to be in *open position* because the interval of the third has been moved up an octave from its location between the root C on the fifth string and the fifth G on the third string, opening a space or gap between the intervals of tonic and fifth. The intervals of this chord are now root, perfect fifth, octave, and tenth (or third), or 1–5–1–3. In measure 5, the E on the first string has been replaced by a G an octave above to create a very open-sounding C chord with the intervals root, fifth, octave, and fifth (or 12th), or 1–5–1–5. (With the E or major third removed the chord is only "implied" major, according to the context.) The chords in measures 1–3 are said to be voiced in *close position* because there are no gaps in the intervals of the C triad. (Some consider *close position* to include chords where there is no space between the upper voices of a chord, but a gap may occur between a single bass note and those upper voices. In this method, we'll adhere to the stricter definition where close-position chords can't have space between any of the notes.)

Play the other chords in the exercise, first strumming each one, and then playing the different voicings as block chords. Note that the close-position voicing for the Am can only be played on the top three strings (in first position). Likewise, the E can only be played in close position on the top four strings. Use the picking-hand thumb for the lowest note of each chord, and the fingers *i*, *m*, and *a* in that order for the notes above it.

Barre Chords

The F in the last system of Example 1 is a barre chord. Barre chords are graphically represented by a Roman numeral above the notes (sometimes preceded by a B) to indicate the fret to be barred. A horizontal dashed line indicates how long to hold the barre, in this case for the duration of the whole note (see also Example 2 in the "Arpeggios" lesson). To play the F barre chord, lay the first finger of the fretting hand across the entire width of the fingerboard at the first fret. Keep the first fretting-hand finger straight but rotated somewhat so that a combination of the side and the face of the finger are in contact with the strings (as shown in the photos below). The remaining three fingers play an E chord shape one fret above where an E is normally played.

To move into this barre chord position, play an E chord using the fretting-hand fingers 3, 4, 2 in place of the usual 2, 3, 1 fingering. Then slide the chord up one fret, and barre across the first fret with the first fretting-hand finger. Getting a clean sound, free of any buzzing, takes some practice. Experiment with the rotation and lateral position of the first fretting-hand finger to see what is comfortable. Barre chords will be discussed at greater length in later lessons, but learning to play the F barre chord will be very useful for playing in the key of C and other keys using first- and second-position chords.

The bracket symbol ([) next to the top two notes of the F chord in measure 23 indicates that the two notes are to be fretted with a single finger, in this case the first finger. To do this, play the F chord in the previous measure, then flatten the first finger by straightening out the fingertip joint and laying it across both the first and second strings at the first fret. The hand may shift slightly when you do this. This move is simplified by keeping the fretting-hand thumb fixed and the palm relatively open.

The position of the barring finger (left) and a full F barre chord (right).

An F chord with a partial barre on the first and second strings.

Voice Leading

When choosing a chord voicing, it's useful to consider how the individual notes (voices) of each chord move throughout the chord progression. This is called *voice leading*. The top note, or voice, of each chord is particularly important because our ears tend to hear that as the melody note, even if there is no explicit melody. Thus, the top voice is key in leading a smooth transition from chord to chord. If the guitar part is an accompaniment for voice or some other melodic instrument, the voice leading should blend with and support the melody. Play the block chord progression in **Example 2** solo and listen to the top voice as it moves from chord to chord. Then play it with another guitarist playing the melody and listen to how the two parts mesh.

Notice how the chords' top voice doubles the note of the melody for emphasis in some places, while at other times it is positioned below the melody note. Generally speaking, the top voice of the chord should not be placed above the pitch of the melody because it will overpower it.

Inversions and Slash Chords

So far we have been using *root position* chord voicings where the lowest pitch of the chord is the root or tonic: the lowest note of the Em has been an E, the lowest note of the C chord a C, and so on. Chords can also be inverted so that one of the other pitches of the chord is voiced as the lowest pitch. Inversions can be used for voice leading and for making better bass lines and smoother chord transitions.

The *first inversion* of a triad is formed by removing the tonic from the bottom of the chord and placing it on top of the chord, thus leaving the third of the triad on the bottom. The *second inversion* is formed by taking the third from the bottom of the first-inversion chord and placing it above the tonic, thus leaving the fifth of the triad on the bottom. For seventh chords, a *third inversion* is made by taking the fifth from the bottom of the second inversion and placing it above the tonic, leaving the seventh on the bottom. Most seventh chords and their inversions are difficult (or impossible) to play in the close positions. For the purpose of illustrating the inversion principle, we'll just use triads in this lesson.

Example 3 shows first and second inversions for some of the chords we have been using. For these particular chords, triad inversions can be easily played in first position (note that the second-inversion E is voiced below the root position and the first inversion). For most chords, however, playing these precise triad

Ex. 2

Ex. 3

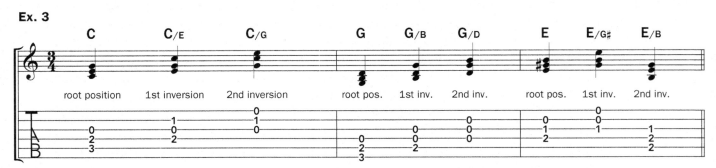

CHORDS AND ARPEGGIOS
Chord Voicings

inversions will require difficult fretting-hand positions, positions higher up the fingerboard, or alternate tunings. For now it's enough to understand the principle of inversions.

Note that the chord symbols written above the notation for the inversions are followed by a slash and then the bass note. For example, the first inversion is written C/E, meaning a C chord with an E in the bass. The second inversion is written C/G, meaning a C chord with a G in the bass. These are called *slash chords*.

Since it's quite common to have more than three notes in a chord, and since it's possible to play slash chords with both open and close positions, the notes above the bass note (slash note) can be rearranged to create a variety of slash chord voicings. It also becomes possible to play slash chords with the seventh in the bass, like C/B♭, G/F, D/C, and E/D. **Example 4** shows a variety of commonly used slash chord voicings.

Ex. 4

Integrating Melody into Chord Progressions

Understanding the concept of chord voice leading makes it easier to begin integrating melodies into a series of chords. In **Example 5,** many of the melody notes are the top voice of the chords. The other notes of the melody are passing tones; these are played while the chord is being held, but are not part of the chord. Before playing Example 5, work through the chords, then play just the melody. Finally, play the melody with the chords, giving a little extra emphasis to the notes of the melody.

Example 5 uses root-position block chords and rolled chords together with a melody in a hymn style. Note that rolled chords are used for dramatic emphasis on the opening chord, the half-note and whole-note chords in measures 3 and 4, the A minor chord in measure 6, and the final chord. Adding some emphasis to melody notes and controlling their note durations will help define the melody. To stop the open-string melody note E in measures 1 and 5, place the *a* finger back down on the first string as you play the following melody note with *m*. The open-string E in measures 3 and 7 can be stopped with the fourth fretting finger using the fretting hand string-damping technique discussed in Example 7 of the "Note Duration" lesson.

In **Example 6**, root-position chords are combined with slash chords to create fluid chord changes with a bass line that is somewhat more arranged than the one in Example 5. Try mixing block and rolled chords using *p, i, m, a* throughout. The picking-hand fingerings are indicated for passing tones in the melody.

Tip: Note that the fretting-hand fingerings have been arranged so the fourth fretting finger is free to damp the open first-string note E while playing the G/B chord on beat three in measure 1. Set the fourth finger down gently but firmly on the open string without plucking it. This is a variation on the fretting-hand string-damping technique. The fourth finger can be slightly flattened to damp the open E of the preceding C chord while playing the G/B on beat two of measure 3. In measure 5, the E string can be stopped with either the fourth fretting-hand finger or the picking-hand *a* finger (though the *a* must move quickly to be in place for the next downbeat). The picking-hand finger *a* can be used to stop the open second string note B in measure 6, because the following three-note chords do not use the *a* finger. Finally, the low E played on the open sixth string in measure 6 can be stopped by lightly touching the sixth string with the second fretting finger while plucking the open A that follows. The second finger must then move quickly to play the note B on the beat four-*and*.

Note that in measure 4 the D chord is held for the whole measure while the quarter-note bass line ascends, or walks up, to the tonic C in the next measure. This type of bass run can be found in many styles of music as a way to complete the turnaround from the dominant V chord back to the tonic or another chord—in this case the IV chord, C.

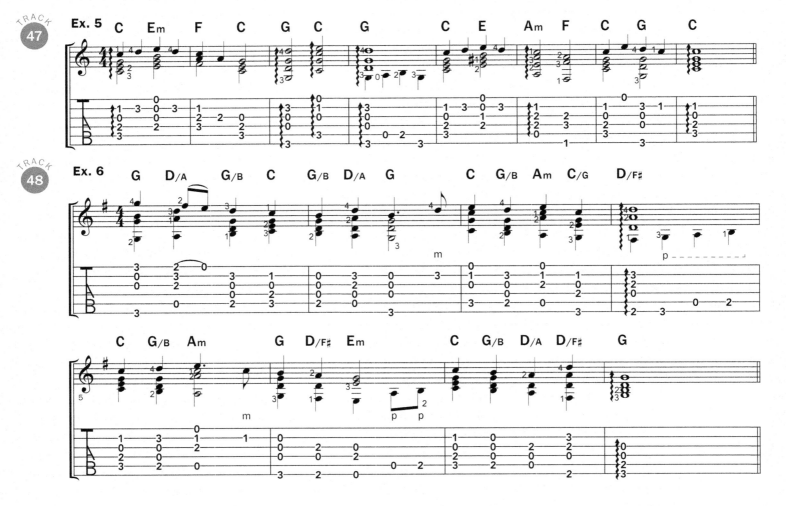

Arpeggios

The word *arpeggio* comes from the Italian *arpeggiare:* "to play the harp." Arpeggios typically outline the notes of a chord by playing the notes in succession in ascending or descending order or some combination of the two. Most commonly used arpeggios are made up of eighth notes or 16th notes, but the notes could have any value. Arpeggios are generally played using free strokes for the fingers, thus allowing the notes of the chord to continue to sound together until the next arpeggio is played. The thumb can play either free strokes or rest strokes (to emphasize the bass notes). However, when the following note is played on an adjacent string, you must use a free stroke to avoid muting that note.

Ascending Arpeggios

To prepare for playing arpeggios, place your picking-hand fingers on the strings. In **Example 1**, the picking-hand fingering *p, i, m, a* is used throughout. After playing each arpeggio, reset the picking-hand thumb and fingers on the strings. This will not only

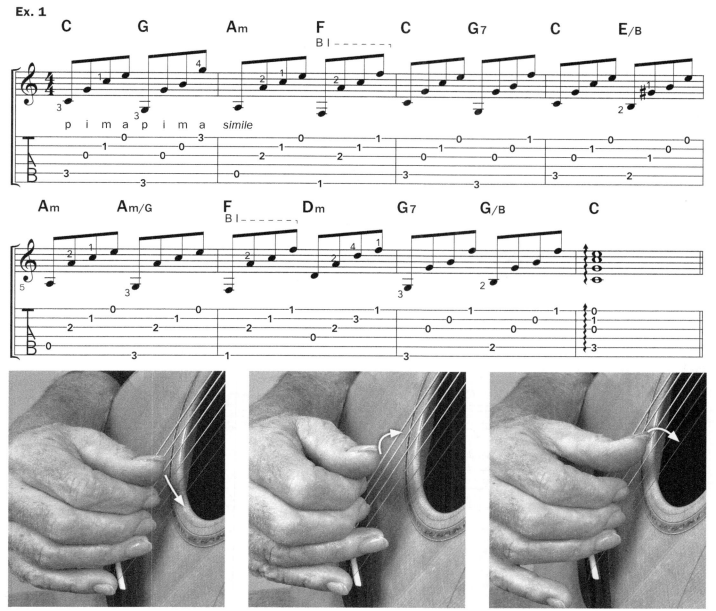

The thumb plucks and resets in a circular motion.

prepare the hand for a fluid execution of the next arpeggio, it will stop any unwanted notes from the previous chord from continuing to sound. It may help to move the thumb in a circular motion to reposition it (see photos on previous page) as the fingers complete the arpeggio.

The fretting-hand fingers remain on the strings until each arpeggio is completed, then they move together as a unit to fret the notes played in the following arpeggio. However, the fretting-hand fingers should continue to hold down notes common to successive arpeggios; lift them only as needed. For example, in measure 5 of Example 1, the first and second arpeggios share the fretted notes C and A on the second and third strings, so the first and second fingers remain down as the third finger frets the G on the sixth string for the second arpeggio. The next two arpeggios also share those notes, so the second finger can remain down while the other fingers are repositioned for the F and D minor chords. The first finger can remain down for the following G and G/B chords. The last chord is rolled, also using *p, i, m, a*.

Arpeggio Bass Lines

Most arpeggios begin with the lowest note that functions as a bass note for the chord. Those bass notes form a moving bass line throughout the progression of arpeggios. Add a little emphasis to them as you play through Example 1, and you will begin to hear that bass line as an independent voice made from a series of half notes. **Example 2** has the exact same notes as Example 1, but the downbeat of each arpeggio has been written as a half note to emphasize the bass line.

Note that slash chord inversions are used in some places to make a smoother transition between the arpeggios.

Descending Arpeggios

There are two types of descending arpeggios. The more common type plays the low note first, followed by the descending notes of the arpeggio. In preparation for **Example 3**, place the fingers on the strings, and begin the arpeggios using *p, a, m, i*. After completing each arpeggio, reset the fingers on the strings in preparation for the following arpeggio to stop unwanted notes from

CHORDS AND ARPEGGIOS
Arpeggios

ringing. Note that the open first string played in the first arpeggio of measure 2 can be stopped using the fourth fretting finger to block it in preparation for the following arpeggio.

We typically think of the low note as anchoring an arpeggio, and therefore it is usually placed on the downbeat, as in Example 3. The other type of descending arpeggio in **Example 4**, where the low note of the chord is played last, is less common but can make for an interesting variation. Use *a, m, i, p*, and as with the previous arpeggios, place the fingers on the strings to be played before beginning the arpeggio. After each arpeggio is played, reset the fingers on the strings in preparation for the following arpeggio. (Since the first three chords have a common bass note, E, try letting the strings ring through the first three chords as an alternative to resetting the picking-hand fingers after each arpeggio.)

Tip: The open-string note E played at the beginning of measure 3 can be stopped at the beginning of the next arpeggio using the fretting-hand string-blocking technique. However, since the the note is common to the following A and E chords, it could be allowed to ring through. Alternatively, you can play the A chord by straightening the fretting-hand third finger across strings 4, 3, and 2 to use the bracketed type of fingering mentioned in Example 1 of "Chord Voicings."

Ascending/Descending Arpeggios

It's very common to combine ascending and descending notes into one arpeggio as in **Example 5**. The picking hand plays the same *p–i–m–a–m–i* pattern throughout the exercise. Prepare each arpeggio by placing *p, i, m, a* on the strings to be played, and reset the fingers only after all six notes of the arpeggio have been completed.

Tip: To stop the open E string played on the downbeat of measure 6, quickly return *p* to the sixth string after playing the open A string at the beginning of measure 7. The same technique can be used to stop the A after playing the open D string at the beginning of measure 8. Practice this move by simply playing the A string and moving the finger back to the E string a few times. After you have the feel, play measures 6–8 a few times, then go back and incorporate the picking-hand string stopping into the exercise.

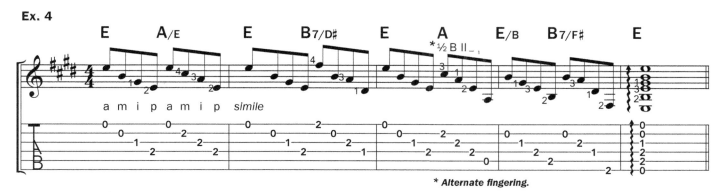

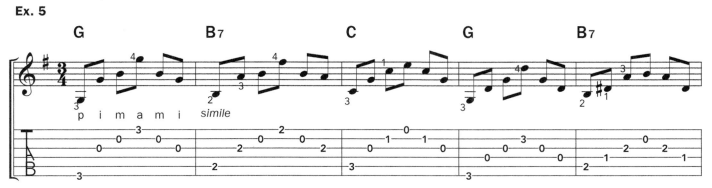

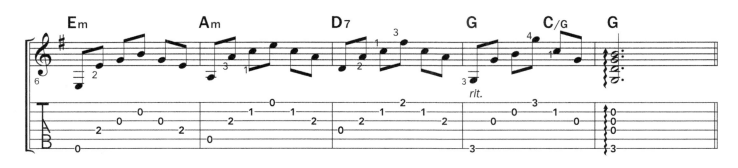

Nonlinear Arpeggios

It's common to mix ascending and descending notes within a single arpeggio to create a nonlinear pattern. In preparation for **Example 6**, place the picking-hand fingers on the strings and play the arpeggio using the fingering *p–i–m–i–a–i–m–i* throughout. Reset the picking hand after each arpeggio (every measure) and emphasize the downbeat of each measure to suggest a moving bass line. Use the same string-stopping techniques as in Example 5 to stop open string bass notes. Then, using the same chord progression, experiment with playing other string sequences.

CHORDS AND ARPEGGIOS
Arpeggios

Arpeggio as Accompaniment
Outlining a chord progression with arpeggios provides a good rhythmic accompaniment for singers and other melodic instruments. **Example 7** is written in two parts; the first part can either be sung or played by a second guitar or other instrument. The picking-hand fingering is indicated *p–i–m–i–a–m*, throughout.

Integrating Melody with Arpeggios
Melodies can be integrated into arpeggios. In **Example 8**, a non-linear arpeggio is slightly modified to accommodate the melody notes played on the top notes of chords. The melody notes on the downbeat of each measure are played simultaneously with the bass notes of the arpeggios using a technique sometimes referred to as a *pinch*. Apply equal pressure to the thumb and the *a* finger of the picking hand as you pinch them toward each other, similar to the action used to play chords. Once you have the feel, try applying more pressure to the melody note to accent it. The other notes of the arpeggio should be played more softly to allow the melody to stand out. The melody can be made to sound more distinct by stopping the open first string on beat three of measures 1 and 3 with the *a* finger as the *m* finger plucks the second string on beat four.

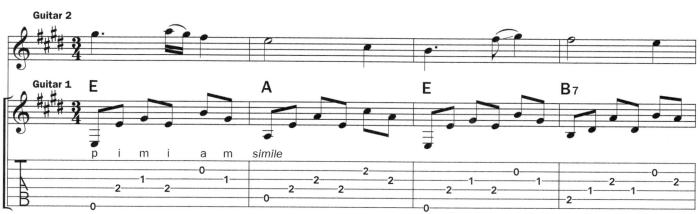

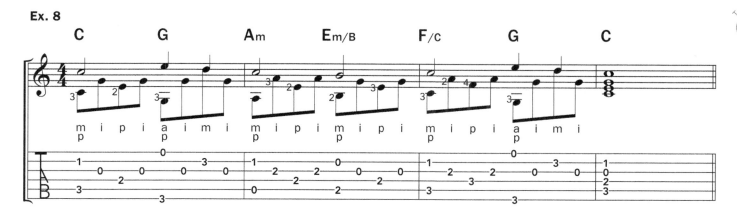

The notes of the melody in **Example 9** change an eighth note before each arpeggio changes. The arpeggios begin on beats one and three of each measure, while the melody notes "anticipate" the beat and continue to sound through the arpeggio that follows. This gives the arpeggios a syncopated, overlapping feel, and helps sustain rhythmic interest throughout the piece—especially when the melody notes are accented. It also requires a little more effort to coordinate the two hands—the fretting hand is often moving an eighth note before the picking hand resets to play the next arpeggio. Alternatively, the melody can be emphasized by resetting the picking hand as the melody note is being played.

In any case, when the picking hand does reset, care must be taken to avoid stopping the anticipated melody note already sounding. The fingerings are tricky, but they have been arranged in an attempt to control the note durations of the melody through a combination of fretting-hand and picking-hand string-stopping techniques. Remember to accent the melody notes and play the other notes of the arpeggio softly, letting them ring until the hand resets to play the next arpeggio.

Ex. 9

64   THE ALEX DE GRASSI FINGERSTYLE GUITAR METHOD

Section 5
Rhythms, Patterns, and Accents

The Alternating Bass 66

Enhancing the Alternating Bass 69

More Patterns 73

Audio Playlist 1, Tracks 58–78

The guitar parts in countless folk, blues, and popular songs are derived from a few common rhythms and fingerpicking patterns. Learning some of these will allow you to play many songs, as well as provide a solid foundation for learning contemporary fingerstyle repertoire, where less traditional rhythms and innovative techniques may use patterns that are not so readily apparent or are even nonexistent. The ability to integrate melodies with these patterns, traditional or otherwise, provides a basis for playing many solo guitar arrangements.

In this section we will cover one of the fundamental patterns in fingerstyle guitar: the alternating bass. We will also look at some other commonly used patterns and rhythms and examine how accents can be used to define and alter them.

The Alternating Bass

Merle Travis is often credited with popularizing the alternating bass in the 1930s as a way to drive his country rhythms. Consequently, the alternating-bass style of fingerpicking is often referred to as *Travis picking*. The idea is to alternate the bass note of each chord on the downbeats, and fill in the upper notes of the chord on the offbeats. The technique has since been adapted to many popular styles of playing. Depending on the time signature, the tempo, and the feel of a piece of music, the alternating bass can be quite versatile. Let's start with the basics.

We'll begin with just the bass line, independent of the rest of the pattern. The thumb alternates continually between two or more strings, depending on the desired bass line. In **Example 1**, the bass notes are arranged such that beats one and three are on the same note, and they alternate with a second note played on beats two and four (the *a–b–a–b* pattern). It's important to learn to play smoothly and in time, applying equal pressure to all the notes. Practice using both free and rest strokes. Following free strokes, try positioning the thumb on the next string just ahead of the beat. This prepares the thumb to pluck the following note with precise timing. With experience, you will come to know which stroke is appropriate to the circumstances. Remember to keep the thumb straight like a lever and initiate the movement from the joint with your hand.

Now that the thumb is getting used to moving from string to string, let's integrate the notes played with the fingers into the pattern. In **Example 2**, use the fingers *i, m,* and *a* for strings 3, 2, and 1, respectively; use *p* for strings 6, 5, and 4 and for the third string on the D chords. Note that the bass notes have down stems and the rest are up stems. That helps separate the two parts

Ex. 1

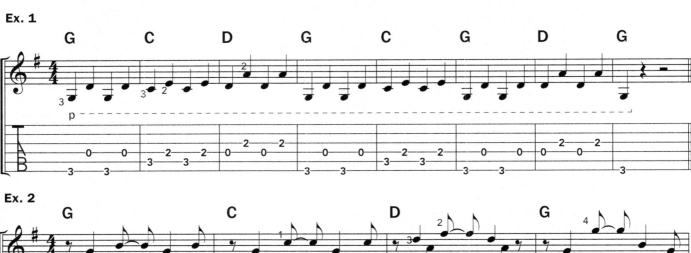

Ex. 2

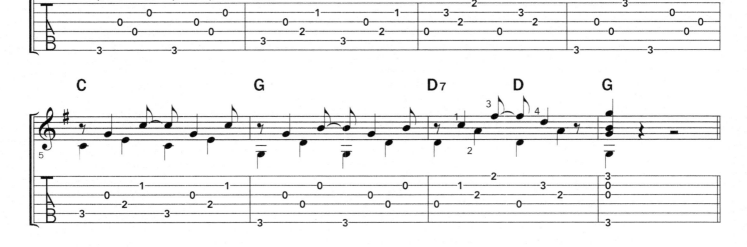

RHYTHMS, PATTERNS, AND ACCENTS
The Alternating Bass

visually, and often, as in this case, determines which notes are played with the thumb and which are played with the fingers.

The fretting hand is playing a chord progression that changes on the downbeat of every measure. As with arpeggios, the notes of an alternating-bass pattern are generally allowed to ring beyond their written value for the duration of the chord being played. As we shall soon see, this is not always the case with the bass notes. But for the moment, try to hold the fretting-hand fingers in position for the entire duration of the measure before changing chords, and reset the picking-hand fingers on the strings at the beginning of each new chord. Some changes make that difficult. Note that in measures 3 and 7, there is a rest on the beat four-*and*, allowing the third finger to release the note D and make the chord change from D to G easier. This is not unusual, and it doesn't impact the rhythm significantly. In fact, it sometimes puts a desirable "breath" in the music—especially in this part of the chord progression where the turnaround V chord (D) resolves to the tonic (G).

Note that a D7 chord at the beginning of measure 7 changes to a normal D chord in the second half of the measure, making for a more final-sounding resolution to the last chord, G. To do this, you need to use the fretting-hand fingering given.

In **Example 3** the alternating-bass pattern in Example 2 has been elaborated by alternating the pitches on beats one and three without changing the pitches played on beats two and four (resulting in an *a–b–c–b* type pattern). Note that sometimes the pitch on the third beat is between that of beats one and two (as in measures 1, 4, 5, and 6). At other times the pitch of beat three is below beats two and four (as in measures 2, 3, and 7). These variations in pitch function like slash chords (see "Chord Voicings") and give greater contour to the bass line.

Accents

Placing an accent on a downbeat, backbeat, or upbeat can completely change the intention of the same sequence of notes. It's important to train the fingers to deliver accents when and where they are called for in the music, rather than letting habit dictate their placement.

In Example 3, an accent mark, graphically represented by the symbol >, has been placed below the bass notes on beats one and three of each measure. Those are the strong beats of the alternating-bass pattern—the ones a bass player might play. Try tapping your foot on beats one and three as you play the pattern, and you will begin to hear a new bass line emerging that might look like **Example 4**. Play this example using rest strokes, holding the note for its full half-note value and taking care to release any fretted notes as you play the note that follows.

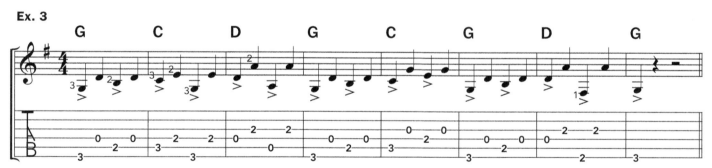

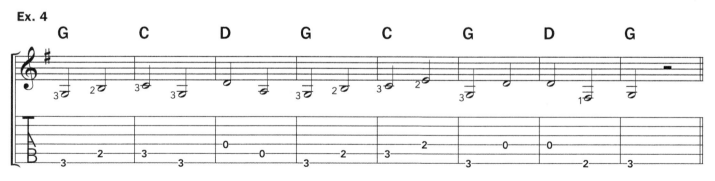

In **Example 5**, the offbeat notes played by the fingers have been added to the alternating-bass line of Example 3. As you practice Example 5, accent the bass notes on beats two and four of each measure, holding those notes for two beats as if they were half notes. Notice how the accents add clarity and definition to the bass line. The notes on beats two and four, the so-called *backbeats*, now take a secondary position in the rhythm, blending in more with the offbeat notes played by the fingers.

Play Example 5 again, accenting beats one and three but releasing them with the fretting-hand finger after their written quarter-note durations (the open string bass notes on beats one and three are difficult to stop, so let them ring—they're all part of the chord). Beats one and three are still dominant, but the feel changes a bit by allowing backbeats two and four and the offbeat notes to "speak" through the pattern more readily. Many transcriptions do not make a distinction on the note durations of the bass notes played—they are usually left to the discretion of the player. Imagine a band where the bass player is playing half notes on beats one and three, and a mandolin player is playing chords on the backbeats two and four, and you can begin to hear (if the tempo is fast enough) the boom-chick/boom-chick rhythm of a bluegrass or country band.

Ex. 5

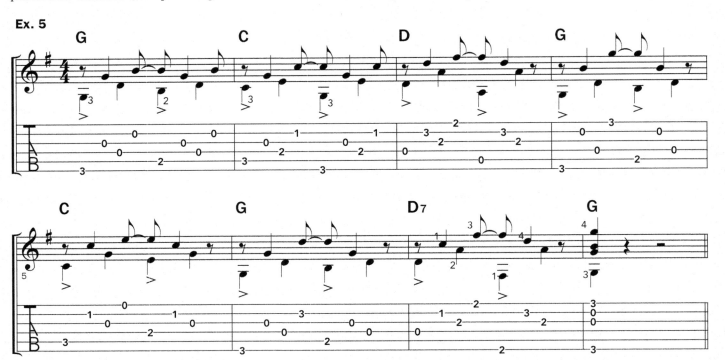

Enhancing the Alternating Bass

Now that you have the fundamentals of the alternating bass under your fingers, let's work on enhancing the sound by adding steps, runs, and pinches, and integrating melody into the picking pattern.

Passing Tones, Steps, and Runs

The chords of an alternating bass pattern can be connected by way of *passing tones* that form *steps* and *runs* in the bass line. Passing tones are notes that don't belong to the chord being played but can be used to add emphasis to chord changes and to create a more contoured bass line. A step is usually one or two notes, and a run is typically longer and often more elaborate. Both are usually accented. In the first measure of **Example 1**, the accented bass notes on beats one, three, and four *step* from G to B by way of the passing tone A. In measure 3 the bass alternates down to the passing tone E on beat three and then steps up to the F♯ on beat four, resulting again in accents on beats one, three, and four. In measure 4, the bass line plays a four-note run by way of the passing tones A and B♭, respectively on beats two and three, resulting in accents on all four notes.

In measure 5, accent beats one, three, and four, using the passing tones B and A to connect to the G in measure 6. A hammered eighth-note step occurs on accented beat three of measure 6. Measure 7 has the same bass line as measure 3, resolving in measure 8 to a solo bass run that employs eighth notes, hammer-ons, and passing tones to embellish the ending.

Note that fewer notes are played on the offbeats with the fingers in Example 1 than in Example 4 in the last lesson. Steps and runs make the picking pattern feel busier, and there's less need to fill all the spaces with offbeats. The run in measure 4 would also sound good without any offbeats being played. Experiment with omitting or adding offbeats to see how it affects the feel of the example. All the down-stem notes are played with *p* and all the up-stem notes (strings 1–3) are played with *i*, *m*, and *a*.

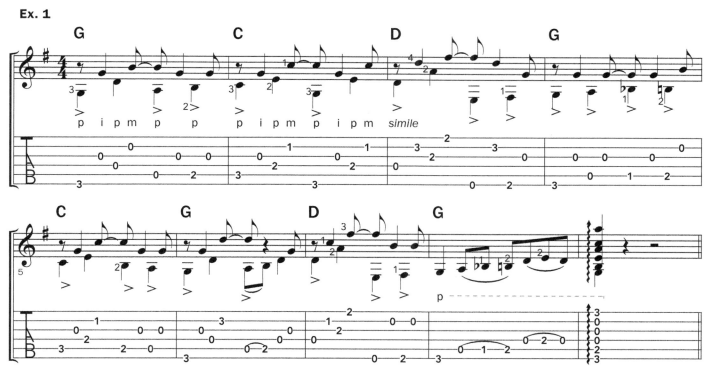

Pinches

The treble notes of an alternating picking pattern can also be played on the beat, together with a bass note, by using the pinching technique introduced in the "Arpeggios" lesson. Apply equal pressure to the thumb and finger of the picking hand as you pinch them toward each other to sound the two notes simultaneously. This pinch works particularly well to emphasize the downbeats of measures as illustrated in **Example 2**. Two notes are also pinched simultaneously on the last beat of measure 7, adding emphasis and a sense of finality to the following chord that ends the phrase. The picking-hand fingers *i*, *m*, and *a* play strings 3, 2, and 1 respectively; and *p* plays strings 6, 5 and 4 and, in measure 3, string 3.

Integrating a Melody

One can hear the beginnings of a melody among the notes played by the fingers in Example 2. By rearranging some of the existing notes and adding a few new ones, a melody can be extracted and integrated into the picking pattern, as shown in **Example 3**. The notes played with the fingers are now divided into two voices: the melody notes, and the remaining off-beat rhythm or "filler" notes. They both have up-stems, but the melody is on top, and

70   THE ALEX DE GRASSI FINGERSTYLE GUITAR METHOD

RHYTHMS, PATTERNS, AND ACCENTS
Enhancing the Alternating Bass

accents have been placed above them (for instructional purposes) to help distinguish the two voices. The filler notes are separated by rests. (This makes the transcription a bit busy, and for that reason many transcriptions you will encounter have been simplified.) By placing strong accents on all the melody notes and de-emphasizing the filler notes, you will notice the melody begin to emerge from the picking pattern. Again, the strong beats one and three of the bass are contoured by steps through passing tones in measures 2, 5, and 6. In those measures the beats one, three, and four are accented. The step in measure 3 has been removed to better support the melody. In measures 2 and 6 the bass has been reinforced by a melody note on beat four.

In addition to accents, controlling the durations of melody notes will give even greater definition to the melody. To execute these precise durations, it is necessary to hold and then release the fretted notes of the melody with the fretting-hand fingers. The open-string E notes on beat one of measures 3 and 5 can be stopped with the picking-hand *a* finger, as can the barred note F on the downbeat of measure 4. (Note that the open-string note E on beat three-*and* of measure 3 is stopped by the fretting-hand first finger playing the barre chord on the downbeat of measure 4, and that the open second-string note, B, on beat four of measure 6 is stopped by fretting the C note on the downbeat of measure 7.) Because the filler notes are played softly, it is not necessary to control their durations.

The pinched melody notes in Example 3 are on the beat, while others melody notes are syncopated, sounding on the off-beats. By shifting the downbeat melody notes to the four-*and* of the preceding measure, a more syncopated feel is achieved in **Example 4**. These melody notes now anticipate the downbeat. The accents (except the pickup note) have been left out of this example, but they should still be placed on the melody notes and the strong beats of the bass. Work on bringing out the melody line.

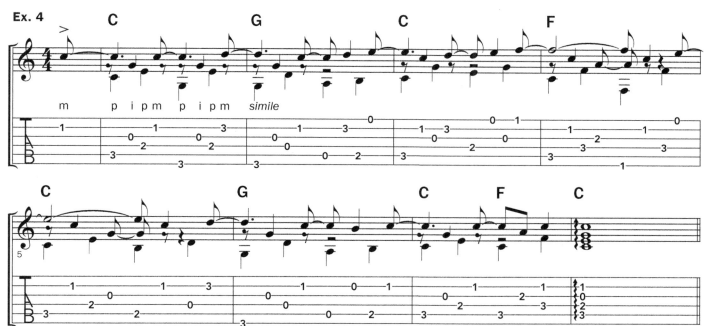

Melodic Independence/Counterpoint

The alternating bass can be integrated with melody in a more contrapuntal style where all the notes belong to either the melody or the bass line. **Example 5** is a country blues. The "filler" rhythmic notes played by the fingers in the previous exercises have been eliminated. It would be possible to add some back in to get a thicker texture, but these notes are no longer necessary to carry the rhythm. The rhythmic interplay between melody and bass has been sufficiently arranged to drive the rhythm, providing a *counterpoint* between the two lines. Example 5 can be played at tempos from slow to medium fast with a *swing* feel (see "Swing Rhythm" below). Pay close attention to note durations. For a more defined sound, the open-string melody notes can be stopped with the picking-hand fingers, and the fretted notes can simply be released.

Notice that the melody uses a variety of note values, and that the rhythmic combinations of notes varies with each measure. This frees the melody from the picking pattern and allows it to develop independently of, but also be supported by, the constant quarter-note alternating bass. For example, the quarter-note G played in the melody on beat four of measure 2 is tied over to the next quarter-note G on the first downbeat of measure 3. The note actually begins when you pluck the eighth-note F♯ on beat three-*and* of measure 2; then you slide up to the G on beat four and hold the note over the bar line.

The rests in measure 3 accentuate the syncopation of the melody. The fretting-hand finger should release the notes ending before the rests for a more defined phrasing of the melody. The melody then continues on the downbeat of measure 4 as a whole note that continues to sound as the bass run is played beneath it. Measure 5 ends with the E on beat four-*and*, anticipating measure 6. Stopping the half note in measure 6 with the *a* finger will allow beats three and four of the bass run beneath it to stand out. Measure 8 modulates to the E major chord and ends with five eighth notes connected by hammer-ons and pull-offs to further break up the feel.

Swing Rhythm

The term *swing* refers to a particular rhythmic feel that derives from blues and jazz traditions. The term *straight eights* is sometimes used to designate a feel that is *not* swung—especially in the context of jazz and blues music. Swung quarter notes retain their normal duration, but eighth notes are counted somewhat unequally; the downbeat eighths are held a little longer and the upbeat eighth notes arrive a little late, more like the third note of an eighth note triplet. The time is still counted 1 *and* 2 *and* 3 *and* 4 *and*, but the *and*s sound on the third note of an eighth-note triplet, as illustrated in **Example 6**. The classic example is a blues shuffle rhythm. Try shuffling your feet next time you get up and walk, and you'll recognize the feel.

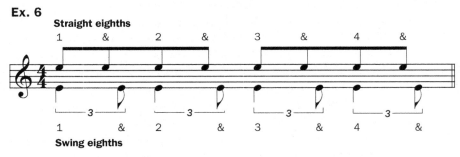

More Patterns

Besides the alternating bass, there are many other commonly used patterns that provide a basis for a variety of rhythms and meters. In this lesson we'll look at patterns in 3/4, 12/8, 6/8, and 2/4 time signatures typically used in blues, jazz, Celtic, and Brazilian rhythms. We'll also continue to explore syncopation and ways of making rhythms swing.

3/4 Time

Travis picking is typically used for rhythms in 4/4, but a variation on the alternating-bass pattern can be used to play the 3/4 rhythm in **Example 1**. The bass line combines some measures of alternating bass (1, 3, 5, 6, and 9) with some measures of steps (2, 4, 7, and 8). This makes for a smoother waltz rhythm. If all the measures had alternating bass, the rhythm might feel jerky and become tiring to the ear. Experiment with rest strokes, releasing fretted notes, and accents to emphasize the individual notes of the bass line. In any case, reset the picking-hand chord every measure to make the chord changes clear. The picking-hand fingering *p–i–p–m–p–i* is used throughout. This rhythm takes on a more country feel when swung—especially at slower tempos.

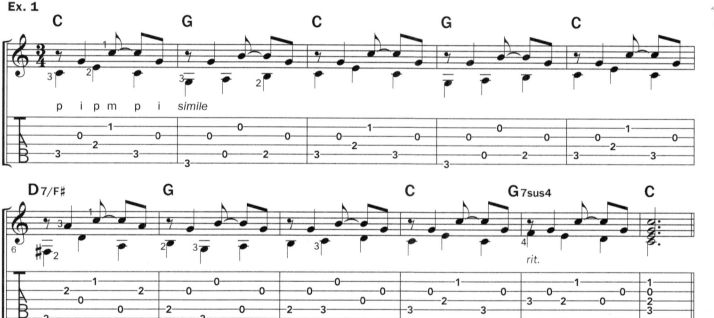

THE ALEX DE GRASSI FINGERSTYLE GUITAR METHOD

Example 2 has the same chord progression but the pattern has been changed. The bass line is not as busy—just dotted half notes in some measures and quarter note steps in others. The up-stem notes are more varied as well, with some on the beat and some on the offbeats. This breaks up the phrasing, adds a sense of space, and emphasizes the waltz feel a little more, especially when tapping your foot on only the downbeats of each measure. This pattern works well at a somewhat faster tempo than the pattern in Example 1.

Syncopated 4/4

A more syncopated variation of a 4/4 rhythm uses a pattern of two dotted quarter notes and a quarter note in the bass, as shown in **Example 3**. This asymmetrical alternating bass groups the eighth notes into two groups of three and one group of two in what is sometimes referred to as a 3–3–2 pattern by playing the bass notes on beats one, two-*and*, and four of each measure. It sounds somewhat like a combination of an alternating bass and an arpeggio. Try counting it: *one, two-and, three, four*. Note that

RHYTHMS, PATTERNS, AND ACCENTS
More Patterns

in measure 3 the fourth beat is divided into two eighth notes connected by a hammer-on to add a little emphasis to the V chord turnaround. In measures 5 and 8, the dotted-quarter bass notes beginning on beat two-*and* are broken into an eighth note and a quarter note connected by a hammer-on, adding a little emphasis to beat three.

Bass and Chord Patterns

Bass lines can be combined with chords to make a variety of rhythmic patterns. The feel and style of **Example 4** is very similar to the feel of the Travis picking used in Example 1 of "Enhancing the Alternating Bass." The bass line is nearly identical, but the fingers play block chords instead of individual notes. Note that the chords are always on beat two or four, replacing the secondary bass notes in the previous example. This bass and chord emphasizes the downbeat/backbeat boom-chick feel that is often heard when flatpickers play country or bluegrass music. Use *p* for all the bass notes (stems down) and *i*, *m*, and *a* for all the chords. The bass note D on beat four of measure 6 can be played with *i*, together with *m* and *a* playing the G and B above it.

Pay close attention to the note durations of chords, bringing the fingers back down on the strings on the rests. Notice how the duration of the chords affects the rhythmic phrasing—the dotted half-note chords smooth out the measures, while the quarter-note chords with rests in between make for a more choppy feel.

Percussive Slaps

A *percussive slap*, sometimes referred to as a slap bass, is a technique wherein the side of the picking-hand thumb slaps one of the bass strings against the frets to create a percussive sound. A percussive slap can be played on both fretted and open strings. It is graphically represented by an *X* on the note head, and by an *X* on the designated string in the tab—the fret number must be deduced from the pitch indicated in the notation.

With the fretting hand off the fingerboard, place fingers *i*, *m*, *a* on strings 4, 3, 2, and place *p* on the sixth string. Keeping the fingers relaxed and in place, use a preloaded stroke of the thumb to pluck the sixth string with the flesh of the thumb. As the thumb follows through with the stroke, raise it directly above the sixth string so it's pointing slightly up and away from the plane of the string (see photo on next page). Then, without moving your hand, slap it down rapidly so the flesh on the side of the thumb tip slaps against the string. If you hold down the thumb long enough to mute the string, only the percussive sound will be heard. If the thumb is released immediately, a note will also sound. In this lesson we will focus on the percussive slap only.

The thumb should remain straight throughout, with all the motion being generated at the thumb joint. This will take some practice, but try to land the thumb so it is in position to pluck the string again, much like you would when executing the picking-hand string-stopping technique with the thumb. If you have nails,

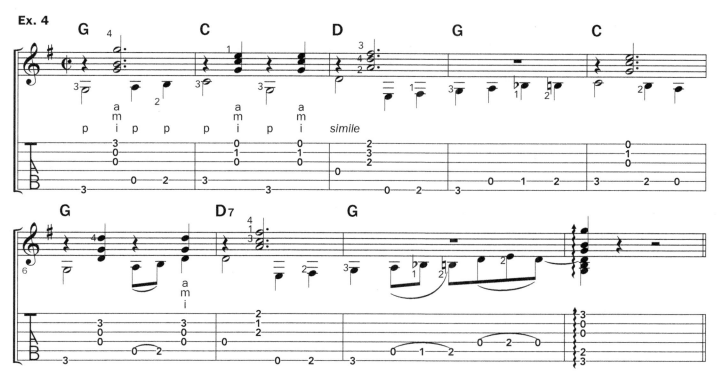

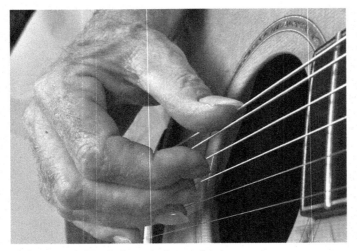

Preload the string before playing a slap bass note.

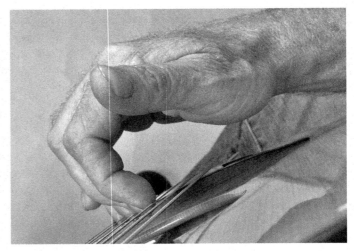

Raise the thumb above the string.

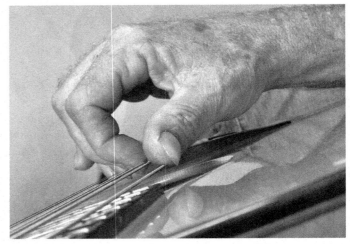

Slap the thumb down rapidly, without smacking the thumbnail against the string.

you'll want to avoid smacking the nail against the string, but have the thumb land close enough to the nail so that you have the choice to use either the flesh or the thumbnail for the following plucked note. If you use a thumbpick, this might be a good time to remove it.

The percussive slap can add a percussive groove to any rhythm, but it is often used on backbeats two and four of medium- and up-tempo pop, rock, and blues rhythms, having an effect not unlike the closed hi-hat or the snare drum. In measures 1 and 2 of **Example 5a** the thumb alternates between a slapped bass on beats two and four and plucked notes on beat one and the upbeat of beat two. (It's easier, and perhaps more common, to use the flesh of the thumb for the plucked notes.) Measure 3 uses all quarter notes, and measure 4 is like measure 1 except beat three is plucked, and the last beat is an eighth-note slap followed by a plucked upbeat note on four-*and* that ties to the downbeat of the

Ex. 5a

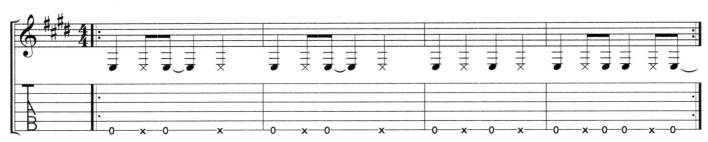

Ex. 5b

RHYTHMS, PATTERNS, AND ACCENTS
More Patterns

repeat. The rhythm is derived from a basic rock drum pattern played on the kick drum (plucked notes) and the snare drum (slapped notes).

Example 5b is a typical rock/blues bass line integrated with the slap bass pattern. Any fretted notes followed by a slap should not be released until after the slap occurs. Likewise, open strings should not be fretted until after the slap. As soon as the slap is executed, the fretting hand can reposition itself for the next note or chord. Note that when the following plucked note is on a different string, as on the last note of measure 4, the thumb should slap that string. This leaves the thumb in position to pluck the correct note, in this case the open sixth string. Practice the line continuously through the repeat with a metronome until you feel the groove.

Example 6 integrates the percussive slap into a bluesy bass and chord pattern. The picking-hand fingers *i, m,* and *a* play the chords, and the thumb plays all the bass notes. Play the grace notes in measures 1 and 3 on the beat simultaneously with the other notes of the chord, then quickly hammer on with the first fretting-hand finger. Pay close attention to the note durations of all the chords, placing the fingers back on the strings to stop them where there are rests. Notice that the eighth-note rest for the chord on beat two of measure 2 occurs simultaneously with the thumb slap. This requires the fingers of the picking hand to come back down together with the thumb as a single unit. The thumb slaps the bass string while the fingers stop the notes of the chord.

The fingers can also join the thumb in a percussive slap, sometimes referred to as a *chord slap*. This occurs on beats two

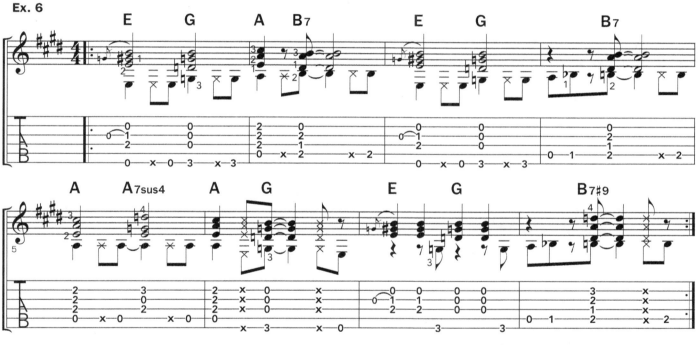

Bend the wrist back without moving the forearm to start a chord slap.

Bring the fingers and thumb down with enough force to press the strings against the frets. Here, the thumb is prepared to play the note following the slap.

and four of measure 6 and beat four of measure 8. Like the bass notes, slapped notes of a chord are represented with an *X* on the note head and an *X* on the designated string in the tab. The picking hand needs to be raised somewhat higher above the strings after playing the preceding chord. Without moving the forearm, raise your whole hand by bending the wrist back slightly, then slap all four strings with *p, i, m,* and *a,* keeping the thumb and fingers together as a unit. As with the thumb, the fingers need to come down with enough force to press the strings against the frets. On beat two of measure 6, the bass note to be slapped is on a different string (the sixth) from the chord that precedes it. The fingers slap strings 2–4, and the thumb slaps the sixth string. On beat four-*and* of measure 8, the fingers stay down on the strings while the thumb plays the pickup note for the repeat. These moves require independent control of thumb and fingers!

The eighth notes in Example 6 can be swung to give a more bluesy feel to the rhythm. Hold the first eighth note for the equivalent of two tied eighth-note triplets, and then play the second eighth note as the third note of an eighth-note triplet. The chords starting on the upbeat (second eighth of beat two) can also be played as if they began on the third triplet of beat two. Sometimes the arranger will simply use the expression mark *swing* to indicate this triplet feel.

In some arrangements, swung eighth notes are written as triplets, as shown in **Example 7**. It's the exact same notes, but the swung notes are shown as triplets. Furthermore, it's possible within a single performance to move between swing and a straight eighth feel.

Try playing the example with and without swing, and experiment with different tempos. Slow- to medium-tempo straight eighths give it more of a rock feel. A slow swing emphasizes the blues shuffle feel, whereas a medium to fast swing starts to sound more like jazz. Try playing measures 1–4 as straight eighths and, without stopping, play the rest with a swing feel.

Triplet Rhythms

Shuffle rhythms and compositions influenced by the blues can also be notated in the time signature 12/8. The quarter note beat is written as a dotted quarter. There are four dotted quarters to the measure, each comprised of three eighth-notes counted as triplets *one*-two-three, *two*-two-three, *three*-two-three, *four*-two-three, with an emphasis on the first triplet of each group. The first two measures of Examples 6 and 7 could be rewritten in 12/8, as shown in **Example 8**.

Triplet rhythms are often used for more up-tempo rhythms as well. **Example 9** is a jig written in 6/8 time. It's similar to the

RHYTHMS, PATTERNS, AND ACCENTS
More Patterns

12/8 time signature, but there are only two beats (dotted quarter gets the beat) per measure, counted *one*-two-three, *two*-two-three. The bass notes play a simple dotted-half-note pattern, punctuated by the occasional eighth-note triplet. In the last measure the chord resolves to the Dm on beat two—anticipating the next measure (the repeat) by a whole beat. (Note that you can stop the open A bass note by immediately returning the picking-hand thumb to the fifth string after playing the open D on the fourth string.) Pay attention to the picking-hand fingerings. The thumb is used to play some of the notes on the third and fourth strings in alternation with combinations *i, m,* and *a* in order to give better definition to the rhythm. Though their cultural origins are different, blues and Celtic rhythms have some commonalities, and it's interesting to note that many contemporary musicians have successfully mixed Celtic rhythms with the blues and with music of Africa. We'll discuss cross-rhythms in a later lesson, but for now, note the contrast of the blues feel in Example 8 with the Celtic rhythm in Example 9.

2/4 Time

The Brazilian rhythms samba and bossa nova are typically played in the bass and chord style, and they are written in a 2/4 time signature. **Example 10** is a ii–V–I–ii–V turnaround using some jazz chords typically found in bossa nova. The bass plays quarter notes on the beat throughout, while the chords add the syncopation. Notice that the chord changes anticipate the downbeats going into measures 2 and 4, as well as between beats one and two of measure 4. This is typical of many Latin American rhythms and is also common in jazz. The bass line is played with *p,* and the chords are played with *i, m,* and *a.* Note that while all of the bass notes are written as full quarter notes, it's actually necessary to release some of them earlier in order to reposition the fretting hand for the next chord. It's not uncommon to see these "impossible to hold" note values in many guitar transcriptions. The intention is that they should function like quarter notes.

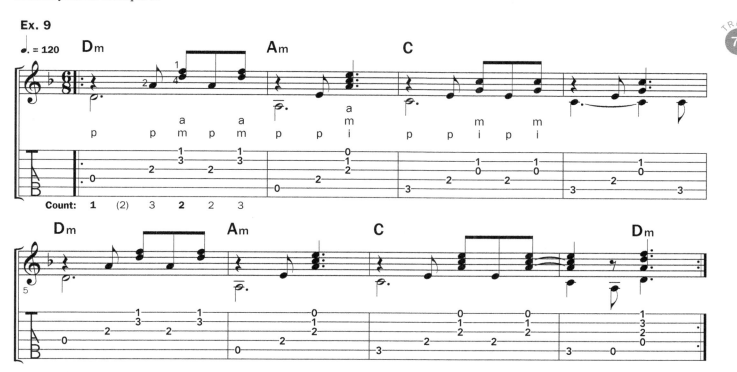

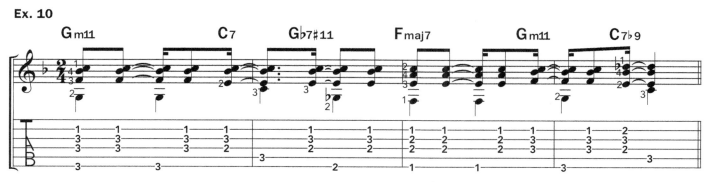

Section 6
Texture

Articulations 82

Vibrato 86

Pizzicato and Harmonics 90

Timbre and Dynamics 98

Audio Playlist 1, Tracks 79–99

Audio Playlist 2, Tracks 1–5

Fingerstyle guitar arrangements gain greater depth and dimension when the sonic texture is enriched. Building texture can make the difference between a flat, two-dimensional performance and one that creates a multi-dimensional sound experience. Articulations, timbre, and dynamics are texture-building tools that offer the guitarist a wide palette of sounds and colors for enhancing the character of individual notes, and for building a dynamic relationship between the different voices—melody, bass, rhythmic accompaniment—that constitute a polyphonic arrangement. In essence, they add dramatic and emotional impact to the music.

This section covers a variety of ways to create texture with fingerstyle guitar, from grace notes and glissandos to vibrato, harmonics, and accents.

Articulations

A wide variety of articulations can be used to manipulate the approach, sustain, and release of an individual note. Articulations can also be used to embellish a melody or to rephrase a bass line. They are not always marked in a score, and their use is often left to the discretion of the player (especially when there is no score!). Building an articulation vocabulary and recognizing where and how to use it can take some effort, but the returns are well worth it.

This lesson introduces a few important types of articulations, including grace notes and legato/staccato techniques. Subsequent lessons will cover other articulations, such as vibrato, bends, pizzicato, and harmonics.

Grace Notes

Grace notes are graphically represented by very small note heads in standard notation, and by small numbers in tablature. They have no real time value or duration of their own. A grace note can be considered both an articulation and an embellishment, because it changes the approach to the note to which it's attached (articulation), and also because it adds a note to the phrase (embellishment). The grace note either steals a tiny bit of time from the note that follows, or it sounds just before the normal note is meant to begin. The duration of a grace note is left to the discretion of the player but generally happens so quickly that it can be difficult to determine whether the grace note begins before or on the beat. In some cases, it might steal a bit of time from each side of the beat. The player needs to be guided by instinct and what feels right in any given situation.

A grace note can be connected to the note that follows via a slide, hammer-on, or pull-off, or it can sound as a completely separate, detached note. The first note of the melody in **Example 1** is preceded by a grace-note slide beginning on the G♯. Pluck the third string (more or less on beat one) while fretting the G♯ at the first fret with the first fretting-hand finger, and then quickly slide the finger up one fret (a half tone) to the second fret to sound the note A without re-plucking the string. Applying a little more pressure toward the fingerboard with the fretting-hand finger while executing the slide will produce more volume and a more defined sound.

There is another half-tone grace-note slide on beat four of measure 5, and a whole-tone grace note slide on beat one of measure 4. Try beginning the grace notes slightly before the beat as well as directly on the beat, and let your ear and sense of rhythm guide you until the timing feels right.

A single hammered grace note occurs on beat three of measure 2. With the second fretting-hand finger at the third fret, pluck the string and then rapidly hammer on the fourth fret to keep the F♯ from sounding for more than a very brief instant.

In measure 2 there are two grace notes played as a double hammer-on leading into the note B on beat one. With the first fretting-hand finger placed on the second fret of the third string, pluck the string and hammer the second and third fretting-hand fingers in a rapid sequence; the second finger hammers onto the third fret, holding down the string just long enough for the third finger to hammer onto the fourth fret, where it continues to hold the B for a quarter note. This should feel like one fluid motion, with the notes A and A♯ sounding so rapidly that it's hard to distinguish the notes from each other. These double hammer-on grace notes lend a relaxed, bluesy quality to the line. They occur again on beat one of measure 3.

There are two grace note pull-offs on beats two and three of measure 5. Again, timing and coordination between the picking-hand and fretting-hand fingers is key. Getting a decisive, crisp pull-off will add clarity and precision to executing grace-note pull-offs.

In measure 5 there is also a grace note preceding beat one that is not connected to the following G. This requires playing two picking-hand strokes (*i, m*) in very rapid succession. To facilitate this, play the first (*i*) stroke with slightly less force than the following (*m*) stroke. To play the grace note on the open string, and then immediately fret it in time to pluck the G, requires precise coordination between the picking-hand and

Ex. 1

TEXTURE
Articulations

fretting-hand fingers. Detached grace notes are often played just before the beat, but practice playing it on the beat as well. Play the whole exercise very slowly and experiment with the timing of all the grace notes.

Legato Embellishments

Hammer-ons, pull-offs, and slides were introduced in an earlier lesson as a way to play notes legato, or connected to one another. We've also seen how they can be used to connect grace notes to the primary notes of a musical line. These legato techniques can also be considered an articulation in themselves—especially when they are used to embellish a musical phrase.

The melody in **Example 2** is very plain, consisting of only half notes and quarter notes. Play it through a few times, using an alternating *i–m* pattern for the picking hand, and reversing the pattern to *m–i* on the repeat. In **Example 3**, embellishments have been added using hammer-ons, pull-offs, and slides to create a more textured and articulated melody with a greater sense of movement and rhythm. Note that the fretting-hand fingering has changed in measures 5 and 6 to accommodate the slide, moving the hand into second position.

Glissandos and Indefinite Slides

Slides of greater length than a whole tone are usually called *glissandos*. Like slides, glissandos are executed with a single fretting-hand finger, and they are graphically represented by either a straight or a squiggly line between the beginning and ending notes. Sometimes they are marked with the abbreviation *gliss.* as well.

In **Example 4**, the melody to the classic blues "St. James Infirmary" begins with a glissando on the last triplet of the pickup measure, starting on the third fret of the third string with the third finger and landing on the downbeat at the seventh fret, four

THE ALEX DE GRASSI FINGERSTYLE GUITAR METHOD

frets and two whole tones higher. This makes for a very dramatic entrance into the melody and sets the tone for the piece. The same move happens at the pickup to measures 3 and 5. Practice the glissandos several times at different tempos, until the motion feels fluid and even. When played very slowly, the individual notes between the B♭ and the D begin to emerge. However, on guitar, it's more typical to play them fast enough so as not to hear the individual notes. Experiment!

Indefinite slides have no fixed starting or ending pitch—they do *not* connect to either a preceding or following note. In Example 4 the notes on beats one and three of measure 1 have indefinite slide symbols pointing downward on the right side. This indicates that the note should be held for all or part of its quarter note value (depending on the player's interpretation), and then begin to fall away in pitch and gradually disappear altogether before the following note is plucked. This "falling away" effect is achieved by sliding the fretting-hand finger toward the nut and gradually, at some indefinite fret, letting up pressure on the string but not releasing it entirely. As the sound dissipates, lift the finger off the string and reposition it (or a different finger, if indicated) to play the next written pitch.

It's up to the player to decide where to stop the slide, but the slides off of beats one and three in measure 1, like the others in measures 3, 4, 5, and 7, should probably go down no more than two or three frets, as the following notes require the fretting hand to be near the starting position. In general, indefinite slides begin to sound too exaggerated if they get much longer.

There's an upward indefinite slide on the approach to beat one in measure 8. This is executed by placing the third fretting-hand finger lightly on the fifth string, plucking the string, and gradually increasing fretting-hand finger pressure as it slides up to the fifth fret. It all happens pretty quickly, but the gradual pressure is what makes the starting pitch indefinite. Practice this slide, initiating the fretting-hand finger contact with the string at different frets. It will probably sound best starting around the third or fourth fret. Experiment starting around the second or even first fret as well.

Staccato

Staccato is Italian for "detached," and the articulation is indicated by a dot (.) above or below the intended note. Staccato is often described as the opposite of legato—the notes feel isolated from each other, even though there are no rests between them. The articulation is normally used on notes of short duration (quarter note or less), and they are not held for their whole value.

Staccato is generally used for fretted notes on guitar, so the fretting-hand finger can release the note well before the next note is played. To get a feel for the articulation, play a series of eighth notes on A, fretting the third string at the second fret and using alternating *m* and *i* strokes. Let up lightly on the string between notes with the fretting-hand finger, so the notes are cut off from one another. Experiment with making the notes longer and shorter. Keeping *p* on the open fifth string will reduce sympathetic resonance.

The familiar French melody "Frère Jacques" in **Example 5** provides a good melody for practicing staccato. The first time through the melody, all the notes are fretted. Use the picking-hand fingerings given, letting up with the fretting hand finger between notes. Note that the first fretting finger plays consecutive notes on different strings. You can facilitate this by keeping the finger fairly flat throughout and lifting the fingertip joint where necessary to release notes, as on the fourth note of measure 1 and the second note of measure 4. (See the text accompanying Example 2 in the "Open Strings vs. Fretted Notes" lesson.)

Ex. 5: "Frère Jacques"

TEXTURE
Articulations

The repeat of the melody in Example 5 (measures 5–8) has been re-fingered so that it is played on a mix of open and fretted strings. To play open strings staccato, it's necessary to stop the note with a picking-hand finger before plucking the next note. When an open string note is followed by another note on the same string (fretted or open), the alternating picking-hand finger stops the string briefly before continuing to pluck it. Practice this by playing staccato quarter notes at a slow tempo on the open B string using alternating *i* and *m* strokes. Pluck the first note with an *m* stroke, then bring flesh of the *i* fingertip down on the string to cut the note short before following through with *i* to pluck the next note. Then bring the *m* finger down to cut off the second note before following through to pluck the third note with *i*, and so on. It's important to use the flesh of the fingertip and not the nail to prevent any clacking sounds and to minimize unwanted noise.

When successive notes are played on different strings, the *same* picking-hand finger used to pluck the open string is used to cut the string short, allowing the alternating picking-hand finger to get into position to play the next note on a different string. This happens in the first half of measure 6, where the third note on the open first string is played with *m*, then *m* is placed back on the string to cut it short before *i* plays the following note on the second string. You may find it easier to return *i* to the second string at the same time; this requires less coordination and leaves *i* in position to play the next note.

A good exercise for practicing this "sticky fingers" technique is to play alternating quarter notes of B and E on the open first and second strings. Using *i* for the second string and *m* for the first string, play the open B, then cut the note short by replacing *i* on the string. Then play the second quarter-note E with *m*, cutting the note short by replacing the *m* finger, and continue alternating. Incidentally, practicing cutting notes short with the picking-hand fingers is a very useful exercise for building speed and accuracy because it trains the picking-hand fingers to get back into position rapidly. These exercises are most useful when played along with a metronome set at a very slow tempo to ensure accuracy. Nevertheless, it's generally simpler and preferable to play staccato on fretted notes wherever possible.

Vibrato

The term *vibrato* comes from the Italian to shake or vibrate, or in the context of playing a musical instrument, to fluctuate the pitch of a note. It is indicated by the symbol ∿ above or below the note, and the technique is typically applied to longer, sustained notes to add movement to a phrase. Traditionally, and more so with nylon-string guitar, the oscillation of the pitch is rapid, but slower vibrato can also be quite effective, especially with steel-string guitars. The rate at which vibrato is applied is called the speed—fast vibratos are indicated with the waves close together, and slow vibratos are indicated with waves spaced further apart. The amount of pitch change is referred to as the depth and may be indicated by the height of the waves.

There are two conventional techniques for employing vibrato on guitar—linear and lateral. Both techniques require a continual stretching and relaxing of the string to make a slight change in pitch. Linear vibrato is applied by stretching and relaxing the string along the length of the string, and lateral vibrato requires pulling or pushing perpendicular to the string (across the width of the fingerboard), then returning it to its original position.

To play a linear vibrato, place the second fretting-hand finger on the seventh fret of the third string to play the note D. The fretting-hand thumb should be placed behind the neck so it lines up somewhere close to the sixth fret. The shoulder and elbow of the fretting-hand arm should be relaxed and free to move. Rock the fretting hand finger back and forth—first toward the nut, then toward the soundhole. The hand rocks back and forth in the same direction as the fretting-hand finger, giving some momentum to the rocking finger. The thumb maintains contact with the back of the neck, pivoting slightly as the finger and hand move.

The fretting-hand finger's point of contact with the string does not change, but the finger will lean one way then the other, causing the string to stretch and then relax. Pressing the finger firmly down on the fingerboard will minimize string squeaks. The pitch goes slightly sharp as it leans toward the nut, returns to normal as the finger becomes vertical, then goes slightly flat as it leans toward the soundhole. The cycle is completed as the pitch returns to normal when the finger returns to the vertical position.

A medium-speed vibrato might pass three or four full cycles of this motion at 60 bpm (three or four times per second). A fast

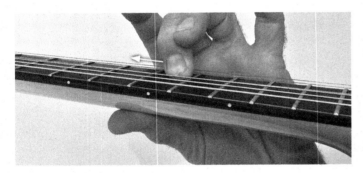

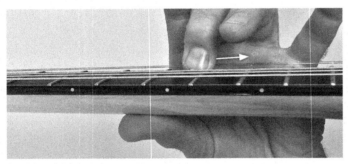

Linear vibrato finger movement is parallel to the string.

Lateral vibrato finger movement is perpendicular to the string.

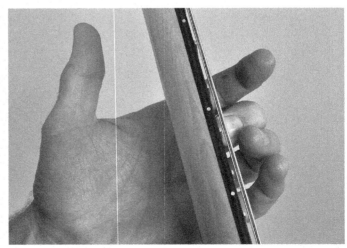

Release the thumb from the neck to play fast or deep vibrato.

TEXTURE
Vibrato

vibrato might have more like six cycles at 60 bpm. The speed can be varied to good effect—starting slowly, then accelerating the oscillations. The more the finger pulls and relaxes (leans), the greater the depth. Linear vibrato is easier and more effective when played at higher positions on the fingerboard where the string is more elastic (because it is farther away from the string's point of attachment). It becomes progressively more difficult approaching the first fret. Try applying linear vibrato at the first fret and then the ninth fret to get a feel for the different elasticity of those positions. Try using each of the four fretting-hand fingers and test it out on all six strings. It may feel easier or more difficult depending on the string as well.

When playing fast and/or deep vibratos, it can be helpful to release the fretting-hand thumb from behind the neck. That allows the wrist and forearm to be more actively engaged in the motion, yielding a more intense vibrato. This is possible when the note receiving vibrato is the only note being played, and when the music allows enough time to free up the hand from having to play other notes.

Lateral vibrato is generally considered easier to use than linear vibrato when playing close to the nut—on the first and second frets in particular—because the string is more pliable in a lateral direction and the pitch changes more readily.

Place the second fretting-hand finger on the second fret of the fourth string and pull the string toward the treble side edge of the fingerboard, then let it return it to its original position. It doesn't take much to fluctuate the pitch, so don't pull it too much! The finger will bend slightly, straightening out as it returns to the original position, but the hand itself does not need to move. Experiment with the number of cycles per beat at 60 bpm, then vary the speed and depth. Unlike linear vibrato, with lateral vibrato the pitch cannot be relaxed below the normal pitch of the fretted note, so it will have a slightly different sound. Try it on different strings and at different positions up and down the fingerboard. The string, and thus the pitch, can be stretched quite a bit using lateral vibrato, especially at higher positions. For this reason is it is also used for the related articulation of string bending.

The notes marked vibrato in **Example 1** are played at different positions on the fingerboard. Use linear vibrato for the first two measures, and lateral vibrato for the lower positions in measures 4–5. Try using both lateral and linear vibrato on F♯ on beat three of measure 3. Experiment with the depth and speed.

Pitch Modulation

A very slow vibrato can be applied to notes to create the effect of *pitch modulation*. The term pitch modulation is normally associated with electronic music, wherein a note from a guitar pickup or electronic instrument is fed to some type of signal processing device like a delay or chorus to vary the pitch electronically. Pitch modulation can be applied with either linear or lateral vibrato at a very slow rate such as 2 or less cycles per second (60 bpm). It can be used so slowly that only a partial cycle occurs during a long note. Because pitch modulation is slow, applying linear pitch modulation at lower positions is easier than with typical vibratos, but the depth of modulation is potentially greater using the lateral vibrato technique. There's no traditional marking for it, but it could be indicated with a fragment of the slow vibrato symbol.

TRACK 84

Ex. 1 Adagio

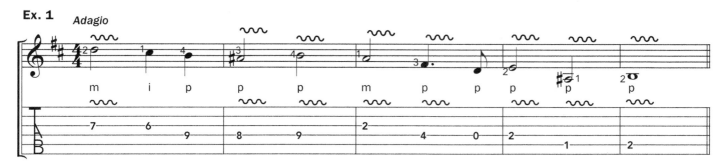

Especially when played slowly, the traditional melody "Amazing Grace" in **Example 2** provides several long notes for experimenting with pitch modulation. This is an articulation that can vary so greatly, that in practice, it's best left to the individual player to decide when to use it and at what speed and depth. Play the melody at 60 bpm and experiment with playing anywhere from a partial cycle to one or two cycles on the notes marked with the pitch modulation symbol. Vary the depth as well. Use a somewhat faster modulation for the quarter note in measure 14 with the traditional vibrato marking. Pay attention to all the other articulations and to the fingerings.

Ultimately the music will sound more interesting if the speed of the pitch modulation is less precisely timed to the beats, and if each note is treated somewhat differently. For example, try waiting till the second beat of a half note to apply a small amount of pitch modulation for some notes, and beginning others with it and stopping after the first beat. Continue to vary the depth of modulation and mix and match linear and lateral vibrato techniques. It can also be effective to start the modulation with the note pulled slightly sharp or flat, and then relaxing the pitch back to normal. This is easier to do in higher positions on the fingerboard. Try re-fingering the melody at a higher position and experiment.

Bends

Bends typically raise or lower the note to a greater degree than either vibrato or pitch modulation. Though they are easier and more often heard on electric guitar, they can be successfully executed on acoustic guitar as well. In music notation, bends are graphically represented by a curved arrow for bends of less than a semitone (such as quarter tones)—upward for a rise in pitch, and downward for a release or lowering of pitch. A bent line is used for bends of a semitone or greater, with individual bent lines used for each bend and release. In tablature, bends are graphically represented by an arrow above the note or notes to be bent, and are often accompanied by a fraction indicating approximately what fraction of a whole tone the pitch is altered. An arrow in each direction means the note should be bent in one direction and then relaxed back to the pitch indicated.

The bending technique is similar to a lateral vibrato. The strings can be bent in either direction, but the fretting-hand finger typically "pushes" the first (and maybe the second) string away from the edge and toward the center of the fingerboard, and "pulls" the sixth (and maybe fifth) string away from the bass side edge of the fingerboard. This keeps those strings from being pushed or pulled off the fingerboard altogether. The middle strings can be either pulled or pushed according to what feels

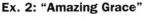

TEXTURE
Vibrato

comfortable in any given situation. Bends are often made with the third or fourth fretting-hand fingers, so that the first and/or second fingers can be placed on the lower part of the string to stabilize the hand for better control. Play **Example 3** very slowly and pay close attention to the note durations and amount of pitch change required for each bend, using your ear to guide you. The first bend on beat two of measure 1 indicates the F is bent up slightly, about a quarter tone, before the following eighth note (G) is played on the first string. Use a metronome set for a very slow tempo, and while counting with a swing feel, sing the pitches *two-and,* where *two* is the F bending up, and G is the *and*.

Some bends, such as the F on the downbeat of measure 2, begin with a *prebend*. This requires preparing the string by pre-bending it a semitone with the third finger before plucking the string to sound the pitch F. The tension is then gradually relaxed to lower the pitch a half step to sound an E on the second eighth note as the string returns to its natural position.

The downward whole-tone bend in measure 5 requires an even greater amount of prebending before plucking the string and relaxing it down from B to A over a period of two eighth notes. The bend was intentionally played on the second string, because bending strings becomes progressively easier at higher positions where the string is more pliable. Gauging the amount to prebend so the pitch begins where you want can only come with experience, so practice the bends in measures 2 and 5 repeatedly till you begin to have a tactile sense of how much tension to exert. Note that the whole-tone downward bend in measure 5 is followed by a pull-off to the G. The bend and the pull-off can be played in one continuous, fluid motion for greater effect.

The bend on the downbeat of measure 3 goes up and down a half tone. The third finger starts at the fifth fret on beat one, bends up to B♭ on beat one-*and,* and then relaxes back down to the A on beat two. (Note that, like the bend in measure 5, this bend is followed by a pull-off.) There is a subtle distinction to be made between a) bending the string continuously for a steady change in pitch, and b) jerking the string more suddenly up or down. Try it both ways, and experiment with everything in between.

In practice, bends, pitch modulation, and vibrato can be combined in various ways to manipulate a single plucked note. The results can be very effective but also difficult to notate, so I encourage you to experiment with combining these three techniques.

Ex. 3

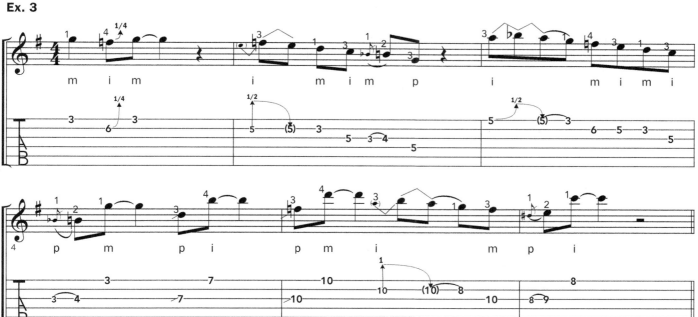

Pizzicato, Muting, and Harmonics

Pizzicato is an articulation generally associated with bowed instruments. It means "plucked" in Italian and is indicated by the marking *pizz*. Since the guitar is normally plucked anyway, the term has more to do with mimicking the sound produced by the *pizzicato* technique on bowed instruments than with how it's actually played on the guitar. On guitar the sound is produced in one of two ways: palm muting (with the picking hand) or fretting-hand muting. Both techniques restrict the string from fully vibrating, thus muting or damping the resonance. Palm muting is generally easier and can be more effective because you can damp all the strings, thereby eliminating any unwanted resonance from the adjacent open strings.

Palm Muting

The palm-muting technique can be used on open strings or fretted notes, and in addition to single-note lines, the damping technique works well for polyphonic playing. Place the heel of the picking hand directly onto the strings over, and slightly in front of, the saddle (see photo). Pluck a few notes with the thumb and listen. The degree of damping is increased by moving the hand toward the soundhole, and reduced by moving the hand toward the saddle.

The damping technique causes the hand to flatten out, thereby reducing the mobility of the fingers somewhat. The thumb is nearly parallel with the strings and the fingers tend to lean downward toward the ground. The hand position tends to favor the thumb, making it a good choice for playing single-note lines across all the strings, as in **Example 1**. It's easier to pluck with the flesh of the thumb in this position, which also takes some of the edge off the sound, further enhancing the muting effect. It takes a little extra effort to get a defined pitch on the unwound first and second strings—especially when they are open. Note that first six measures of the melody are played in third position. The fingering changes to second position on the last note of measure 6 for the remainder of the arrangement. This fingering allows most of the notes to be played as fretted notes, avoiding the open first and second strings.

The picking hand can cover all six strings, as in Example 1, or just the bass strings, leaving the top two or three strings either partially or entirely undamped. This works particularly well with Travis picking and other types of picking patterns. The *thump-a-thump* sonic quality of the bass becomes differentiated from the ringing sound of the melody played on the top strings, allowing for two distinct voices that enhance the polyphonic nature of the arrangement. Play **Example 2** with the heel of the picking hand covering just the bottom three strings, so the top strings are free to ring out. Note the that the third string is not used. It can be a bit of a "no-man's land" because it's a challenge to keep it consistently either damped or undamped. Use *p* for strings 4–6, *a* for the first string, and *m* for the second string.

The basic principle of lever and hinge still applies, but the hand has to adapt to a new position, so it takes some practice. You may find it helpful to hold your fingers away from the strings a little when they are not plucking a string, thus helping to keep that side of the hand raised off the upper strings. With time and practice, this becomes more instinctual. Once you've got the feel of it, try moving your hand closer to or farther away from the saddle to vary the amount of damping on the bass.

Fretting-Hand Muting

Fretting-hand muting is achieved by pressing the string down directly over the fret with the fretting-hand finger, so that both the

Two views of the palm-muting hand position.

TEXTURE
Pizzicato, Muting, and Harmonics

finger and the string touch the fret. That prevents the note from ever developing a full sound, instead producing a somewhat muted sound. It is indicated by the marking *F.M.*, with a dashed line indicating which notes are to be muted. The articulation is normally used with short notes, and the fretting finger is typically lifted soon after the string is plucked, adding a staccato quality, though it is possible to sustain longer notes. Because the strings not being played are not muted, there will, unlike with palm muting, continue to be some resonance. This may or may not be desirable, depending on the music, but it can add an interesting background, reverb-like texture. Experiment!

Ex. 1

Ex. 2

* Downstemmed (thumb) notes only.

Try a few fretting-hand muted notes, then play the melody in **Example 3**, muting only the notes indicated. It takes some practice to land the fingers directly on the fret, though the technique is somewhat easier to execute on the wound strings (3–6), because they are wider and the texture of the winding requires a little less precision in placing the fretting-hand fingers. The example sounds good with background resonance from undamped strings, but as an alternative, the first finger can play a partial barre at the second fret across the top four strings while muted notes are being played. This reduces resonance from those strings and makes the fingering somewhat easier. To eliminate background resonance altogether, barre the finger across all the strings. There are also two sets of picking-hand fingerings—try them both.

Fretting-hand muting requires a good deal of practice. It can be quite difficult to sustain for long passages or scale runs or at fast tempos, because the fingers are displaced from their normal position in order to land directly on the frets. For this reason, fretting-hand muting is often used for single notes, short passages, or, as in Example 3, repetition of a few notes to establish a rhythmic motif.

Harmonics

The term *harmonic* refers to a note consisting only of overtones produced by dividing the vibrating length of the string into equal parts. The harmonic is graphically represented in the notation by a diamond-shaped note head. It is represented in the tablature by a dot after the fret number, and sometimes by the fret number in parentheses or some type of enclosure. Sometimes the abbreviation *Harm.* is placed over the fret numbers. Harmonics extend the upper range of the guitar—beyond the notes available on the fingerboard—and they also allow the guitarist to play pitches that are otherwise too high to reach while holding lower fretting-hand positions. They have a distinct texture that is often described as sparkly, bell-like, or ephemeral—harmonics are sometimes referred to as chimes. They generally have greater impact when used sparingly and in contrast to normal notes. There are two fundamental types of harmonics—*natural* and *artificial*.

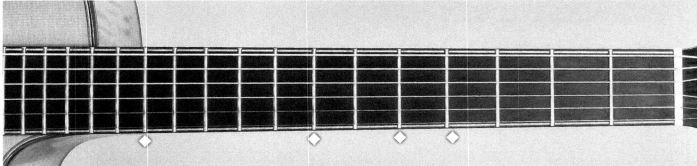

Natural harmonic nodes are found at the 12th, seventh, fifth, and fourth frets.

TEXTURE
Pizzicato, Muting, and Harmonics

Natural harmonics are produced at specific locations, or *nodes*, that divide an open string into equal parts. The pitch is determined by the number of divisions. Dividing the string in half at the 12th fret produces the first harmonic; dividing the string into three parts at the seventh fret produces the second harmonic; dividing the string into four parts at the fifth fret produces the third harmonic; and so on. The pitches and tab for all the natural harmonics at each of the first four harmonic positions are notated in **Example 4a**. Note that because some of the pitches are very high, the symbol *8va* is used to indicate notes that sound one octave higher than they are written.

Place either the third or fourth fretting-hand finger so it rests lightly across all six strings at the 12th fret. (You can use any finger, but it's good to get in the habit of using the third and fourth fingers, especially in the higher positions because those are the fingers often used in practice.) Rest the pad of the finger lightly on the sixth string without pressing it down. Pluck the string with the picking-hand thumb and then immediately lift the fretting-hand finger off the string. This should produce a bell-like sound. If the harmonic does not sound, try using either more or less pressure with the fretting-hand finger, and experiment with how quickly you lift the fretting-hand finger off the string after plucking it. Be sure the fretting-hand finger is directly over the fret (you may need to move it slightly toward the nut or the soundhole). The technique requires good timing and coordination between fretting-hand and picking-hand fingers to produce a good, solid tone.

The pitch produced by playing the first harmonic at the 12th fret is one octave above the pitch of the open string—the same pitch (in this case E) as the note produced by normal fretting of the sixth string at the 12th fret, or the fourth string at the second fret. Try playing the first harmonic at the 12th fret on all six strings by drawing your fretting-hand finger toward the treble side, leaving the string just played uncovered and free to ring as you place the pad of the finger over the next string and pluck it. Once you get the feel, try playing all six harmonics simultaneously with a quick strum as the finger rests across the strings. The coordination between the fretting-hand finger and the strum needs to be timed so that the finger lifts off of each individual string just after it's been strummed.

Using the same technique, play the second harmonic at the seventh fret on all six strings. The pitch of the second harmonic, shown in measure 2, is a fifth higher than the one played at the 12th fret (B on the sixth string), making it an octave plus a fifth—or a 12th—higher than the open string. Now play the third harmonic at the fifth fret of each string using the second fretting-hand finger. This produces a pitch an octave higher than the first harmonic, or two octaves above the pitch of the open string, as shown in measure 3.

The first three harmonics all line up neatly with the frets, but the fourth harmonic is played slightly behind (toward the nut) the fourth fret. The pitch produced is a third above the third harmonic, or two octaves plus a third above the open string, as shown in measure 4. It takes more accuracy and perhaps a bit more fretting finger pressure to produce clear fourth harmonics on the unwound first and second strings. A slower release of the fretting finger on those strings can also help. The fourth harmonic can also be produced at the ninth fret. For reasons too complex to go into here, the fourth and higher harmonics do not line up with any of the frets. The fifth and higher harmonics become more difficult to locate accurately, and it is difficult to produce a clear sound. For these reasons, they are less frequently used and have not been notated here. But with a little experimentation, you will discover their locations.

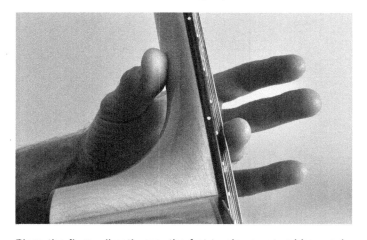

Place the finger directly over the fret to play a natural harmonic at the 12th fret.

Ex. 4a

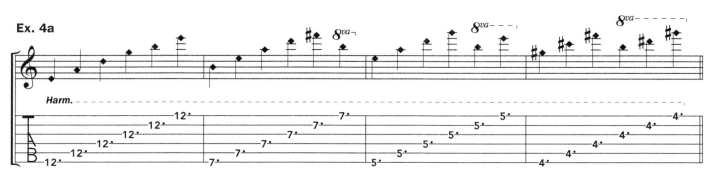

The pitches of each open string and its first four harmonics are notated in **Example 4b**. Play each open string followed by the series of ascending harmonics on that string a few times to get a better sense of how the pitches progress on a single string. Use the fretting-hand fingerings given to get some practice using all four fingers for harmonics. This fingering also reduces "travel"—the amount of repositioning the fretting hand must do.

As demonstrated in **Example 5**, harmonics can be used to play individual notes (measures 1 and 3), an entire melodic phrase (measures 8 and 9), and even chords (measure 10). Even though the exercise is to be played very slowly (marked *lento*), the fretting hand needs to move quickly and accurately from the ninth to the second fretting-hand positions after playing the harmonic at the beginning of measures 1 and 3. Practice making this move at a very slow but steady tempo. Looping each measure as if there were a one-measure repeat will help you get the flow. This will take some practice but is well worth the effort as many harmonics require fretting hand position shifts. The minor position shifts in measure 9 are relatively easy, but take care to avoid touching the strings already sounding harmonics so that they ring through the measure. This can be achieved by positioning the fretting fingers more perpendicular to the fingerboard and touching the harmonic nodes with the fingertips of the fretting fingers.

The harmonics G and F# in measure 8 illustrate how you can access very high harmonic notes while the fretting hand is in a lower position (the entire phrase in measure 8 is played with the fretting hand in second position). To play the first chord in measure 10, lay the third fretting-hand finger across the top five strings and pluck the middle four strings with *p, i, m, a*, taking care to let the open sixth string continue to ring. As the harmonics continue to ring, the harmonic (B) on beat two of measure 10 is played with the fourth finger. Then the third finger is placed across the top four strings to play the final harmonic chord. Only the top three strings (and the sixth string) are plucked, but the fretting-hand finger stops the fourth string, allowing the harmonic previously played on the fifth string to continue to sound with the chord.

Ex. 4b

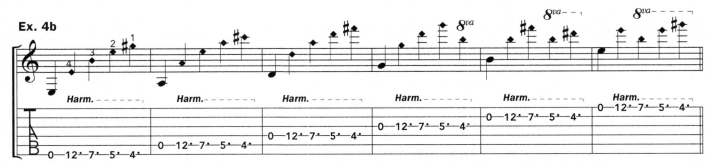

Ex. 5 Lento

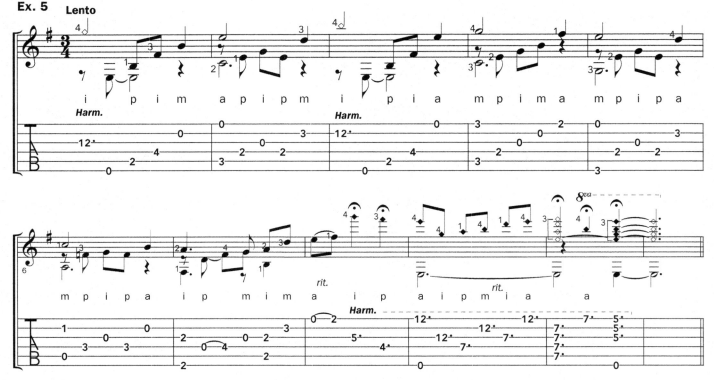

TEXTURE
Pizzicato, Muting, and Harmonics

Remember that all notes marked *8va* sound an octave higher than written. Note that the highest harmonic note (E) of the final chord extends beyond the range of notes available on the fingerboard.

Artificial Harmonics

Like natural harmonics, artificial harmonics are produced at nodes that divide the string into equal parts—the differences being that artificial harmonics are played on fretted rather than open strings, and that the picking hand touches the harmonic node. Artificial or picking-hand harmonics are graphically represented in the notation by the same diamond-shaped note head accompanied by the text *P.H. Harmonics* or *P.H. Harm.* above the tab. In the tab they are represented by a fret number indicating the position of the fretting finger, followed by a second number in parentheses indicating the fret where the node occurs. Because the string length is adjusted by fretting, artificial harmonics are available for all the notes of the chromatic scale.

Artificial harmonics are usually played by touching the string 12 frets above the fretted note—this is the location of the first harmonic. The second, third, and fourth harmonics can also be sounded by touching the string seven, five, or four frets above the fretted note. For example, to play the first harmonic octave of the pitch F, the fretting finger is placed at the first fret of the sixth string and the node is at the 13th fret. The second, third, and fourth harmonic nodes are found at the eighth, sixth, and fifth frets respectively. The picking-hand index finger is outstretched at an angle to the string, with the pad of the fingertip resting on the node. Pluck the string with either the picking-hand thumb or the *a* finger, and then immediately lift the index finger off the string (see photo). (Note that natural harmonics can also be played on open strings using this technique.) Practice locating the nodes and getting a good clear sound by playing the chromatic scale in **Example 6**.

A good way to orient your hands for finding artificial harmonic nodes is by fretting familiar chord shapes while playing

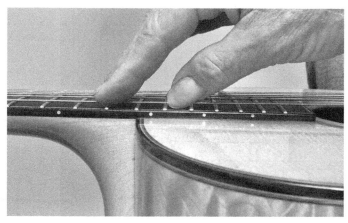

The fretting-hand index finger is placed on the node and the thumb plucks the string for an artificial harmonic at the 13th fret.

Ex. 6

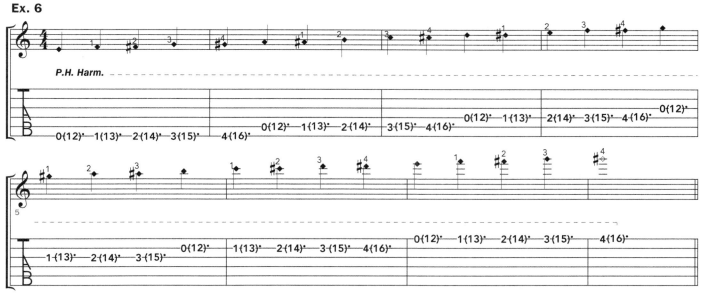

THE ALEX DE GRASSI FINGERSTYLE GUITAR METHOD

arpeggios with the picking hand, as in **Example 7**. Let the notes ring for each chord, and let up on the fretting hand just enough to stop the chord before releasing the strings altogether. This will avoid any unwanted sounds. Let the open strings ring throughout. The last three notes of the exercise are played at the second, third, and fourth harmonic nodes on the third string.

Artificial harmonics can be integrated with nonharmonic notes. In these situations it's preferable to use the *a* finger to pluck the string, so the thumb is free to pluck notes. **Example 8** shows a simple blues lick using harmonics in the melody and a combination of open and fretted notes in the bass. Note that harmonics can be bent just like normal notes, as shown in measures 1 and 3. A grace-note slide is used on the harmonic on beat three of measure 3, causing the harmonic to be combined with the fundamental pitch. Try to hold the short bass notes to their written value by stopping them with the thumb.

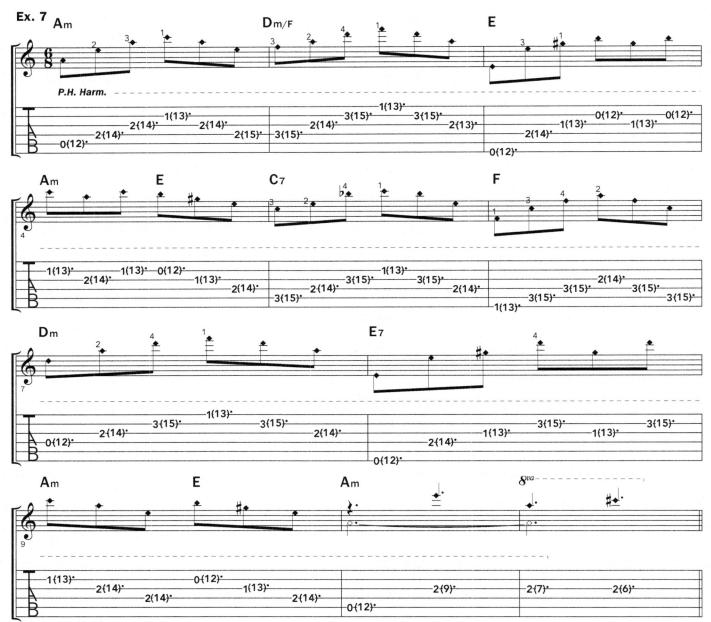

96 THE ALEX DE GRASSI FINGERSTYLE GUITAR METHOD

TEXTURE
Pizzicato, Muting, and Harmonics

Ex. 8

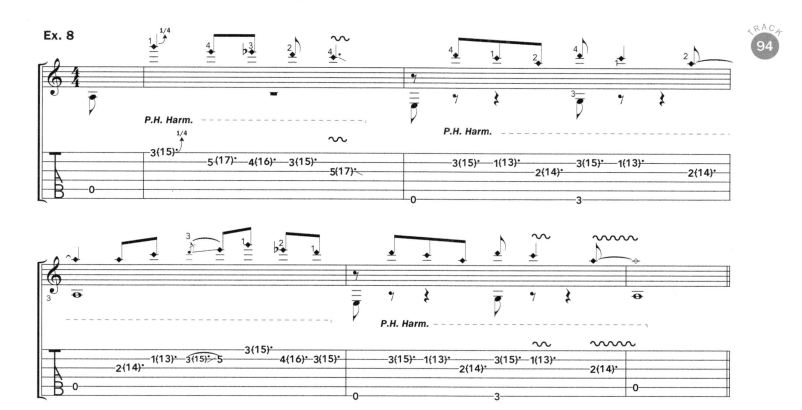

THE ALEX DE GRASSI FINGERSTYLE GUITAR METHOD

Timbre and Dynamics

The French term *timbre* is often used interchangeably with the English term "tone color." The articulations discussed so far alter the shape and texture of notes played, whereas timbre typically refers to how the overall tone is shaded—as in a drawing or photograph—regardless of the articulation. Is it warm and dark or bright and metallic? For example, when you listen to recorded music, you may hear a wide variety of sounds and textures but you can still adjust the brightness or darkness of the music using tone controls. Likewise, a fundamental timbre can be applied to any of the textures discussed above.

Timbre is most typically expressed on the guitar by the position of the picking hand in relationship to the bridge and soundhole. Playing toward the fingerboard side of the soundhole emphasizes the fundamental tone and yields a warmer, darker sound called *sul tasto* (Italian for "below the fret"). Playing toward the bridge emphasizes the attack and higher overtones, yielding a edgier, steelier, and brighter sound known as either *ponticello* (Italian for the bridge of a musical instrument) or *metalico* (Spanish for metallic). Working between these two poles allows the player to accentuate and contrast individual notes and phrases.

Play the arpeggios in **Example 1** and gradually move your hand from *sul tasto* position (near the fingerboard) in measure 1 down to *metalico* position (near the bridge) as you approach measure 4. Repeat the phrase and reverse the movement—moving from *metalico* to *sul tasto*. Listen to how the gradual change in timbre adds a sense of movement to what is otherwise a fairly repetitive phrase. The change in timbre also directs more attention to the one accented note in each measure—that note moves back and forth between F♯ and E, but it sounds different each time. Play those notes alone, rearranged in measures 5 and 6, and listen to the movement as the hand travels from *sul tasto* to *ponticello*.

TRACK 95

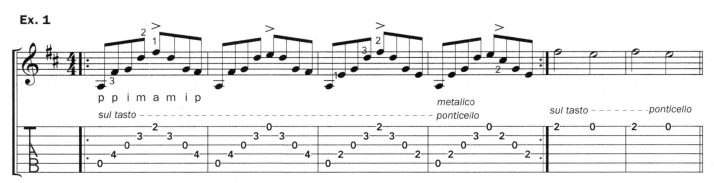
Ex. 1

Picking hand in *sul tasto* position.

Picking hand in *metalico* position.

TEXTURE
Timbre and Dynamics

Playing *sul tasto* can be effective in expressing sweetness, intimacy, or mystery. It works well at slow tempos, at the end of phrases, and in exposed passages where the darker sound is not overshadowed by other notes in the music. In **Example 2**, the final phrase of the traditional melody "Greensleeves," is shaded from *metalico* to *sul tasto* gradually over the course of eight measures. The darker *sul tasto* sound amplifies the sense of mystery of the final chord (is it major or minor?).

Playing *metalico* is good for achieving a more aggressive sound and also very useful for clarifying and adding definition to a rapid succession of notes or any passage that is sounding a bit muddy. This is especially true with a line like the one in **Example 3** where the pitches are also in the low register. The picking-hand fingerings have been carefully chosen to allow you to apply string-stopping techniques—controlling note durations will also help clarify the line.

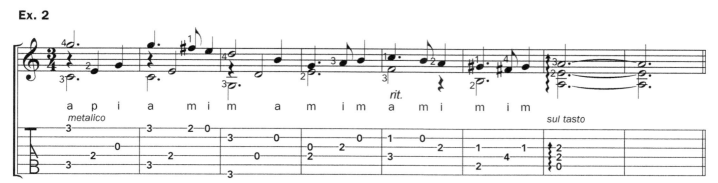

More sudden shifts in timbre can be employed to differentiate between voices in the music. This lends itself quite well to the classic musical device of *call and response*, where a short phrase (or part of a phrase) played in one voice is answered, or echoed, by a phrase in a second voice. Sometimes, the response is referred to as a *countermelody*. In **Example 4**, the first and second notes of each phrase in the melody are answered by the third and fourth notes of each phrase. For example, the pickup measure note G and the F# on beat one, measure 1, are answered by the melody notes D and B in measures 2 and 3, and so on. By assigning a different timbre to each group of notes, you can emphasize the sense of call and response. Play the call *metalico* and the response *sul tasto*, and try to hear the dialogue between the two parts, or voices, of the melody. The effect is increased when the "call" is played loud and the "response" is played somewhat softer. Note that the second note of the call continues to sound through the response, creating an "overlapping" effect. By returning the picking hand to a more central position (slightly to the bridge side of the soundhole) for the last melody note of measure 6 and the final chord in measure 7, you create a sense that the two voices (call and response) have merged at the end of the piece. Try playing the passage with the timbre markings reversed; play the call *sul tasto* and the response *metalico*. Experiment!

Flesh vs. Nails

A fundamental difference in tone can be produced by using either the nail or the flesh of the picking-hand thumb and fingers. Plucking the strings with the nail alone accentuates the attack and the higher harmonics, yielding a brighter tone. Using the flesh of the thumb and fingers reduces the attack and higher harmonics, yielding a softer or smoother sound. There are many gradations of tone that can be produced by strokes combining both flesh and nail. Anything is possible, but it's typically easier to use only the flesh of the thumb than only the flesh of the fingers (assuming the player has nails). For this reason, we will concentrate on the use of these techniques with the thumb.

Plucking the strings with the flesh of the thumb can be effective in softening the sound of a bass line, thereby allowing the melody or other lines in the music to "speak" more clearly. To avoid catching any nail, use the pad of the thumb. This is facilitated by slightly lowering the picking hand so the thumb becomes more parallel to the strings. In this position, the thumb can easily play a *non*-preloaded stroke to further soften the sound.

Move the thumb parallel to the strings to play a non-preloaded stroke for a softened sound.

Ex. 4 *Moderato*

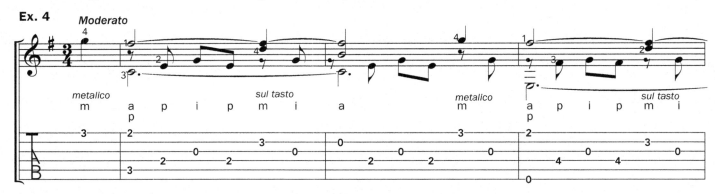

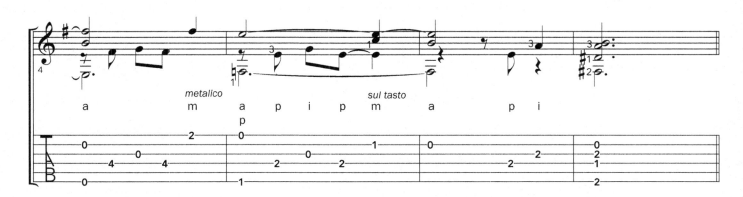

TEXTURE
Timbre and Dynamics

Play the first four measures of the bass line in **Example 5** with just the flesh of the picking-hand thumb. For measures 5 and 6, switch to playing with the thumbnail. This change allows the bass note of the chord to be more easily heard, and also allows the bass line turnaround that follows to be featured more prominently. Switch back to the flesh of the thumb at the repeat. Note that measures 5 and 6 are also marked *metalico* to give more "bite" to the chord and the bass feature. The *i* finger can be used on the fourth string in measure 6, but those notes can also be played with the thumb. Try it both ways.

Dynamics and Accents

The term *dynamics* refers to the range of volume levels used to enhance the expression of music. Dynamics are indicated primarily by the use of the Italian words *piano* (*p*) meaning soft, *forte* (*f*) meaning loud or strong, and *mezzo* (*m*) meaning half or medium volume. These three abbreviations can combined in a variety of ways to give finer gradations of volume levels like *mezzo-forte* (*mf*) for medium-soft, *fff* for as loud as possible, etc. The terms *Sforzando* (*sfz*) or *subito piano* are used to indicate a sudden increase or decrease in volume. Crescendos and decrescendos—increasing or decreasing volume over time—are graphically represented by the "hairpin" symbols.

Dynamics can be a very powerful tool in performance. Soft passages have the power to draw the listener in, and loud passages can get the listener fired up. The impact of dynamics is often most powerful when used in contrast. For example, a soft passage comes as relief to a loud passage, and a loud passage can come as the culmination of a long-building crescendo that began with very soft notes. As with fast and slow tempos, a whole concert of only loud or only quiet music can become a bit static.

It is therefore important to develop a big dynamic range and to be able to get a clean, balanced sound at any volume. The techniques on rest strokes and preloading the strings for maximum tone and volume presented in "The Picking Hand" are something even the seasoned player should never cease to improve on. Likewise, learning to play very softly but precisely will increase your dynamic range and provide an expanded palette for creative expression. Play the repetitive chord exercise in **Example 6** with a steady crescendo (increase) and decrescendo (decrease) in volume as indicated by the hairpins and the dynamic markings. Practice making the *pp* as soft as possible and the *ff* as loud as possible while still making all the notes of the chord sound evenly and cleanly at a steady tempo.

Ex. 5

Ex. 6

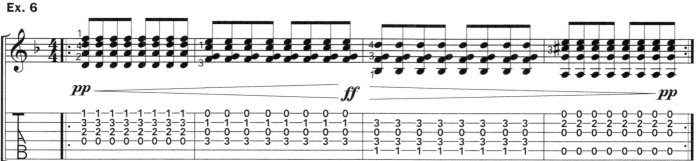

THE ALEX DE GRASSI FINGERSTYLE GUITAR METHOD

Dynamic markings have been placed into the musical excerpt in **Example 7** (note the sixth string is turned down to D). The piece begins moderately softly (*mp*) and becomes even softer (decrescendo) through measure 4, where it is marked *piano (p)*. At measure 5, the volume should increase (crescendo) rapidly to a very loud *ff* in measure 7. Measure 8 is marked *subito p* (suddenly quiet), in stark contrast to measure 7; and then the chord in measure 9 is marked *pp*, indicating that the piece should end very softly. Note the ritard and accelerando markings—slight variations in tempo add emphasis to the dynamic changes.

Traditionally, dynamics are applied sequentially to contrast one passage with another, or to add a sudden emphasis on a particular note or chord. However, dynamics can also be applied continuously by way of accents to contrast different voices with each other. We noted in Example 4 that the call-and-response mechanism defined by contrasting timbres can be further accentuated by playing the call (*metalico*) much louder than the answer (*sul tasto*). These sorts of "internal" dynamics are hardly ever marked—it is a matter of learning to choose which notes to accent and which notes to de-emphasize. As you apply the sequential dynamics marked in Example 7, try also to emphasize the melody so that it always sounds louder than the softly played accompaniment notes of the broken arpeggio. Using accents as a way of applying internal dynamics is a powerful tool that we will continue to explore in future lessons.

Ex. 7
Dropped-D Tuning: D A D G B E

TEXTURE
Timbre and Dynamics

The Water Is Wide

Now that we have covered a variety of texture-building tools, let's combine them in some complete songs. Slower tempos often allow the player to focus more on articulations, timbre, and dynamics, so we'll begin with the traditional ballad "The Water is Wide."

In **Example 8** the melody is stated in its plainest, unadorned form. Each note of the melody is plucked separately, and no articulations have been applied. Learn the melody, paying close attention to the picking-hand and fretting-hand fingering given and experimenting with rest strokes and preloaded free strokes to get the best tone possible. Note that the whole melody is played in second position, and the fretting-hand fingers clearly outline a D chord.

Ex. 8: "The Water Is Wide"

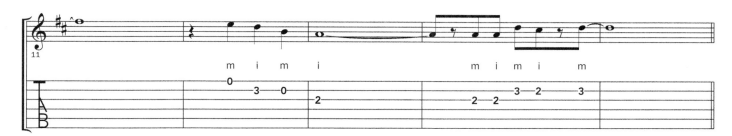

In **Example 9**, the melody has been rearranged to include an accompaniment complete with articulations, dynamics, and timbre markings. It's in cut time—the time signature is 4/4 but the pulse is felt on the half note, so tap your foot and set the metronome to somewhere around ♩=52. The sixth string is tuned down to D. Though the rhythm is slow, it is propelled along by syncopations (anticipated notes) in both the melody (measures 4, 6, 8, 10, 12, and 14) and, occasionally, in the bass lines (as in measures 3 and 13). There is a third, stems-down, countermelody voice that answers the melody (measures 5, 7, 9, 11, and 15), and it should have a dynamic level well below the melody.

Pay close attention to the fingerings, articulations, and timbre and dynamic markings. It might be helpful to work on just the melody, then add the bass notes, then work on the third voice. Measures 9–12 may be somewhat challenging for the fretting hand, so give that passage some extra care. Remember to let the harmonics in measures 1 and 3 ring free, and apply a light slap to the bass notes marked X in measure 13. Once you've learned the piece, experiment with some articulations, timbres, and dynamics of your own.

Auld Lang Syne

The classic Scottish melody "Auld Lang Syne," often sung at midnight on New Year's Eve, has been arranged in **Example 10** in a British Isles folk and blues style (the embellishments might even suggest the sound of a bagpipe). The first time through the melody (measures 1–15) is marked *andante* (♩=88), but it sounds good even slower as well and it should be played somewhat freely as indicated. There's a slight pause at the fermata at the end of measure 15, then the tempo changes to *allegro* (approx. ♩=138), introducing the slap bass (presented in "More Patterns") to add some syncopation and rhythmic drive. In measures 1, 10, and 18, the first eighth note of the tied melody on beat two has been embellished. It is now a 16th note followed by rapid 32nd note hammer-ons and pull-offs. It may help to count (use the metronome!) eighth notes as quarter notes at about half tempo to work out the timing before bringing these embellishments up to speed. The precise timing of the 32nd notes is not critical—what's important is landing on the following eighth note in time.

A third voice occasionally fills in where there are long notes in the melody, as in measures 5, 11, 15, 32, 34, and 36. Keep the volume of these fills a little softer than the main melody. In measures 15 the bass line plays off the third voice by way of a "delayed" slide. The bass note C and the third voice note E are played together on beat three, the third voice pulls off on the three-*and*, and then the bass note slides on beat four to double up the note D. A similar thing happens in measure 32—this time the third voice hammers onto E on beat two, the bass note is played on two-*and*, and then the third voice pulls off at the exact same time that the bass note slides to D on beat three-*and*—again doubling the note D.

Use lateral vibrato (or pitch modulation) on notes marked vibrato (at the second fret). It becomes challenging to play vibrato where the fretting hand is holding other notes as in measures 9 and 26, particularly when the tempo picks up. Try adding a very slow pitch modulation to the high E in measure 4 and any other long notes. Pay attention to all articulations, timbre, and dynamic markings and experiment with your own.

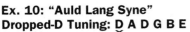

Ex. 10: "Auld Lang Syne"
Dropped-D Tuning: D A D G B E

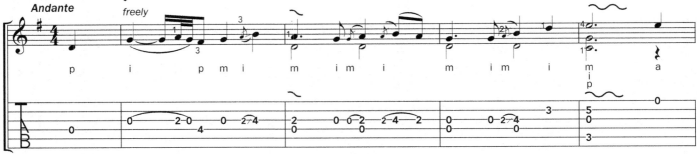

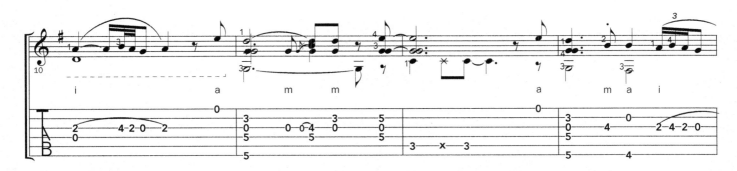

TEXTURE
Timbre and Dynamics

Section 7
Moving Up the Fingerboard

Cross-String Techniques 110

Barre Chords and Cross-String Arpeggios 116

Audio Playlist 2, Tracks 6–22

Playing beyond the first and second positions opens up many new doors. It not only expands the range of the instrument but presents a whole new landscape for integrating multiple voices and textures. The nonsequential relationship between those pitches fretted beyond the fifth fret and those found on open strings requires some new tools for navigating the fingerboard. In this section we'll explore the use of cross-string techniques for playing bass lines, melodies, and arpeggios. We'll also look at barre chords and partial barre chords and ways to integrate them in fingerstyle arrangements.

Cross-String Techniques

Cross-string techniques provide powerful tools for fingerstyle guitar. Perhaps most importantly, they allow the player to integrate single lines (melodies, bass lines, etc.) using picking-hand positions and patterns similar to those used to play arpeggios, alternating bass patterns, and chords. Distinct from the alternating *i–m* pattern introduced in the lesson "The Picking Hand," the cross-string technique allows the fingers to be used in opposition with the thumb to play these lines. The cross-string technique also provides flexibility for creating texture, accents, and determining note durations by using open strings in alternation, and in contrast to, fretted notes.

Played in first and second positions, the notes of ascending or descending lines progress sequentially from string to string. This is true for fingerings utilizing open strings as well as for those using only fretted notes. For example, an ascending G-minor scale played entirely in first position using open strings progresses sequentially from the sixth to fifth, fourth, third, second, and first string and back down again, as illustrated in **Example 1**. In first position, the string sequence used to play the scale is: 6, 5, 5, 5, 4, 4, 4, 3, 3, 3, 2, 2, 2, 1, 1, 1, 2, 2, 2, 3, 3, 3, 4, 4, 4, 5, 5, 5, 6, 6, 6.

In second position, the scale becomes more challenging to play because there are several notes that require a fretting-hand *extension*—a fretting-hand finger stretching one fret out of or beyond position. In particular, the first fretting-hand finger must stretch to reach the notes B♭ on the fifth string, E♭ on the fourth string, and the F on the first and sixth strings. This is true whether or not open strings are used, as illustrated in **Example 2**. As in Example 1, the notes of both these second-position fingerings progress sequentially up and down the strings as well.

In third position or higher, it becomes possible to combine open and fretted strings to play ascending/descending intervals

Ex. 1

Ex. 2

MOVING UP THE FINGERBOARD
Cross-String Techniques

on nonsequential strings. This technique is called *cross-string picking*. For comparison, first play the third-position G-minor scale in **Example 3**, which uses all fretted notes. Then, play the third-position cross-string G-minor scale in **Example 4**. The sequence of strings used to play the ascending scale is now 6, 5, 6, 5, 4, 5, 4, 3, 4, 3, 3, 2, 2, 2, 1, 1, 1. The first ten notes of the scale (6, 5, 6, 5, 4, 5, 4, 3, 4, 3) alternate strings back and forth from lower to higher to lower again. (Looking at the tablature is a good way to visualize the cross-string sequence.) Once the B♭ is played on the third string, however, the remainder of the notes in the scale, as with Example 1, progress sequentially from lower to higher strings. This is because the pitches of the top two open strings, B and E, are not part of the Gm scale, so it's not possible to utilize the cross-string technique in this part of the scale. To match the more legato texture of cross-string playing, these notes are connected to each other by hammer-ons and pull-offs.

Compare the picking-hand fingerings for Examples 1, 2, and 3 with those in Example 4. In Examples 1 through 3, *p* plays all the notes on strings 6–4, and the notes on strings 3–1 are played using alternating *i* and *m* strokes. (The alternate fingering shown below in Examples 1 through 3, often used for classical guitar, uses alternating *m* and *i* throughout.) The picking-hand fingering for the cross-string scale in Example 4 moves back and forth between *p, i, m,* and *a* fingers. Though a "single line" is being played, the alternation of thumb and fingers feels more integrated with the picking-hand patterns used to play the alternating bass, arpeggios, and chords found in many fingerstyle arrangements.

In Example 4, note that the fourth finger is required to extend beyond normal third position to reach the note A at the seventh fret on the downbeat of measure 2. This extension is made somewhat easier for the fretting hand because the preceding note G is played on an open string, allowing the first finger to release the F at the third fret before the fourth finger extends to play the A.

Picking-Hand Position Shifts

The fingering in Example 4 requires a *picking-hand position shift* in order to continue playing the scale with a fingerstyle feel. For example, the first five notes of the scale are played with *p* on the sixth string, *i* on the fifth string, and *m* on the fourth string. To play the next three notes, beginning with the sixth note (E♭), the picking hand shifts position so that *p* plays the fifth string, *i* plays the fourth string, and *m* plays the third string. Beginning with the

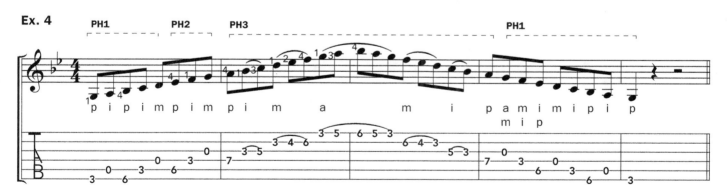

note A on the downbeat of the second measure, the picking hand shifts again so that *p* plays the fourth string, *i* plays the third string, *m* plays the second string, and *a* plays the first string. These three different picking-hand positions are designated with the symbols PH1, PH2, or PH3 below a dashed line spanning the notes to be played in the designated picking-hand position. These markings are for instructional purposes only and are not normally found in guitar transcriptions.

The picking-hand fingering for descending the scale is slightly different than for the ascending scale. Beginning with the note G in the fourth measure, the picking hand jumps directly from PH3 to PH1. This allows the open G string to be played with *a*, leaving that finger in position with the option to stop that string as *m* plays the F on the string below. (Stopping the open G while ascending is not an issue because both fretting hand and picking hand will stop it to play the next notes.)

It's possible to stop the G string with *m* in the PH2 position; however, it would require more effort for the *m* finger to play the open third string, stop it, then reposition itself to the fourth string in the PH1 position in time to play the D on beat three. Try both picking-hand fingerings and experiment with picking-hand string stopping to hold notes to their written eighth-note values as well as allowing the open strings to ring. Listen to the difference.

Getting a feel for picking-hand position shifts and understanding the logic behind them will help you navigate through cross-string technique. Try singing the notes of the scale, and with the fretting hand off the fingerboard, practice moving the picking hand from PH1 to PH2 to PH3 and back to PH1 at the appropriate moment. Notice that shifts are sometimes on a downbeat and sometimes on an upbeat. This will vary with the line being played. Also, picking-hand positions are not always so clearly defined as the ones in Example 3. In some situations the fingers of the picking-hand fingers will be separated by more than a string. This is especially true when playing chords and arpeggios and occasionally when playing melodic lines.

Fretting-Hand Position Shifts

Sometimes a line played cross-string will also require a *fretting-hand position shift*. This is particularly true of scales like E minor that use all six open strings. In **Example 5**, the scale shifts from second to fourth position after the first three notes and from fourth to tenth position at the end of measure 2. These three

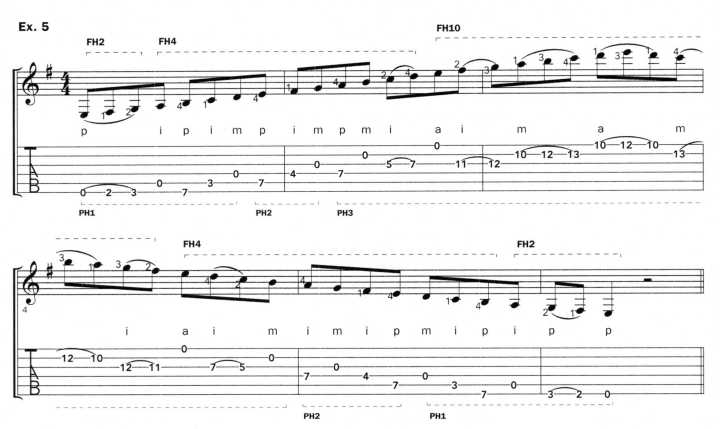

MOVING UP THE FINGERBOARD
Cross-String Techniques

fretting-hand positions are designated with the symbols FH2, FH4, and FH10 over a dashed line spanning the notes to be played in the designated fretting-hand position. (As with the picking-hand position markings, these fretting-hand markings are for instructional purposes only.) Note that the position changes begin on an open string, allowing the hand to arrive at the new position in time to play the next fretted notes.

Fretting-hand position shifts may seem like an extra effort at first, but they offer many benefits. The shifts actually facilitate extending the scale to a full three octaves. Fretting-hand shifts also provide an opportunity to add some interesting phrasing and articulation along the way. In **Example 6**, the traditional cowboy tune "Streets of Laredo" is played cross-string beginning at the seventh position. When the fretting hand shifts down to third position in measure 4, it provides an opportunity for the fourth finger to make an indefinite slide (ending somewhere around the seventh fret) from the C played on the last beat of measure 3 while the next note is being played on the open B string.

In measure 4, the open string G on beat two provides contrast to the following fretted G. In measure 8 the fourth finger glissandos all the way back up on a grace note to resume the melody at the seventh position. In the next-to-last measure, the open string B is doubled up with a fretted B on the fourth string to emphasize the ritard at the cadence. The final C chord is strummed at the seventh position where vibrato is easily applied. All of the these moves modulate the phrasing and add textural contrast to the line.

When allowed to ring freely, the contrast of overlapping open and fretted notes gives the phrasing a harp-like quality (cross-string playing is sometimes referred to as harp style). It's also possible to control all the note durations for a more defined sound. Allowing the fretted notes to overlap slightly before releasing them can give a fluid, legato quality to the phrasing. As you play the example, experiment with note durations of both open strings and fretted notes and explore the textural possibilities.

Ex. 6: "Streets of Laredo"

Rhythmic Patterns and Phrasing

Cross-string playing can also be combined very effectively with accents to outline a rhythmic structure. The accents in **Example 7a** outline a syncopated dotted-eighth, dotted-eighth, eighth-note rhythm n 4/4. It's counted "<u>one</u>-ee-and-<u>a</u> two-ee-<u>and</u>-a." The first two measures of the picking-hand pattern are the same—*p, i, m, p, i, m, p, i*—and all the accented notes are played with *p*. The pattern is altered in subsequent measures to position the picking-hand fingers so they can stop open strings and control note durations. However, the accents continue to fall on *p* strokes until the last beat of measure 7 and into measure 8, where accents are shifted to the *i* and *m* fingers for the higher notes. To maintain the rhythmic pattern, the picking-hand sensitivity needs to adjust quickly to change the pattern and deliver the accents with the fingers. Experiment with the alternate picking-hand fingerings below.

A variety of phrasings and musical intentions can be produced by manipulating the accents and note durations. As you play Example 7a, observe the accents but try to hold all the notes to their written 16th-note value. This can be done by letting up briefly on all fretted notes and using picking-hand damping to stop any open strings. Once you get the feel, experiment with playing the notes staccato or *tenuto* (held for their full value) to vary the texture. Contrast that with letting all the notes ring.

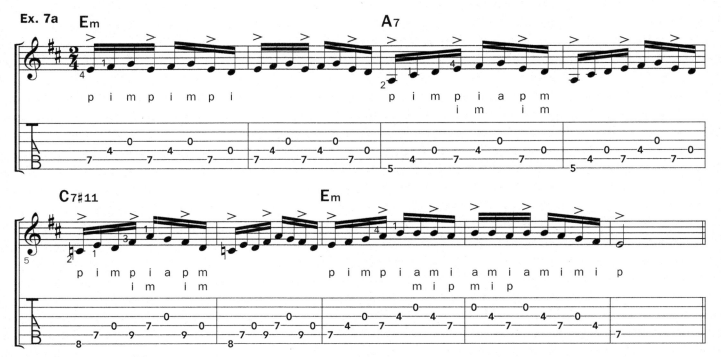

MOVING UP THE FINGERBOARD
Cross-String Techniques

In **Example 7b** the same accented notes are held for a full dotted-eighth, dotted-eighth, eighth pattern. For example, in the first measure, don't lift the fourth finger, but continue to let up on the first finger and damp the open G as the next note is played. Played this way, the accented E notes can begin to sound like a different voice—perhaps a bass line. Try playing only the accented notes as well. That will help you feel the rhythm and hear the proper note values.

In **Example 7c**, the accents are moved to different notes in the sequence, bringing out a second voice with new note durations in the upper part of the pattern. The lower notes in the sequence should be de-emphasized somewhat to allow the new line to speak through. Note that the picking-hand fingering is now *p, i, m, p, i, m, p, i* throughout. The notes played on the open strings are allowed to ring but can still be stopped at the rests to control note durations accordingly.

THE ALEX DE GRASSI FINGERSTYLE GUITAR METHOD

Barre Chords and Cross-String Arpeggios

A first-position barre chord (F) was introduced in the "Chord Voicings" lesson. The barre is used to hold down two or more notes at the same fret with a single finger. It is graphically represented by a Roman numeral preceded by a B placed above the note or chord where the barre begins. A dashed line to the right indicates how long the barre is held. There are two fundamental types of barre chords: full barres, where the first fretting-hand finger frets across all six strings; and partial barres, where the finger frets anywhere between two and five strings.

Full barre chords can be moved anywhere on the fretboard because they do not use open strings. For example, the same fingering used for the F barre chord introduced in the "Chord Voicings" lesson can be moved one fret higher to play the same voicing in F♯, up two frets to play the same voicing in G, and so on. It might help to think of the barring finger as a temporary capo that relocates with each full barre. Theoretically, any chord that can be played in first or second position that leaves the first finger free can be played a half tone or higher up the fingerboard as a barre chord. However, some of those chords might require difficult stretches.

Example 1 shows some of the commonly used major, minor, seventh, and sus chords built on the first-position E, A, and C chord shapes. Since they are fully movable, try them out at different frets and learn to identify them.

Common Chord Voicings

In standard tuning, many first- and second-position chords that incorporate one or more open strings might include the root, third, fifth, and seventh to get a 1–3–5–7 or 1–5–7–3 voicing. An additional "color" interval such as a ninth, 11th, or 13th might be added by dropping the third or the fifth to get voicings like 1–3–7–9 or 1–5–7–9, or even 1–3–7–9–11 or 1–3–6–9. These types of chords are less likely to use open strings and generally require all four fretting-hand fingers. To a great extent, barre chords are good for playing either 1–5–7–3 or 1–7–3–5 type voicings that may add an 11th or 13th in place of the third or the fifth. (Any of the above voicings may include pitches doubled in different octaves.)

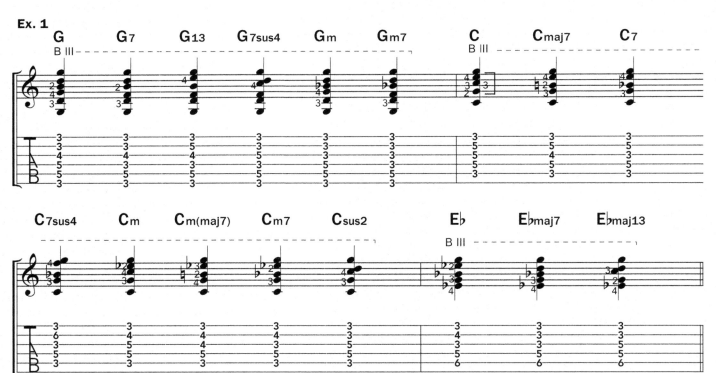

Ex. 1

116 THE ALEX DE GRASSI FINGERSTYLE GUITAR METHOD

MOVING UP THE FINGERBOARD
Barre Chords

Full barre chords are convenient for strumming rhythm-guitar parts, as shown in the first four measures of **Example 2**. Note that the Fmaj in measure 4 is not a barre chord, but it can be strummed across all six strings with the first finger muting the open fifth string. Plucking blocked or rolled chords allows you to be more selective about the voice leading and to avoid any barred notes that are not part of the chord, as shown in measures 5–8. The G13/A♭ is also not a barre chord.

Partial Barres

Partial barre chords are formed one of two ways: 1) by raising the part of the finger nearest the hand to uncover one or more of the top strings, or 2) by laying the finger flat across the fingerboard but leaving one or more of the lower strings uncovered (see photo). The Roman numeral above the partial barre is preceded by a fraction, indicating how many strings are to be barred. Some transcriptions simply use 1/2 to indicate any type of partial barre. In some cases the fraction indicates greater detail like 1/3 or 2/6

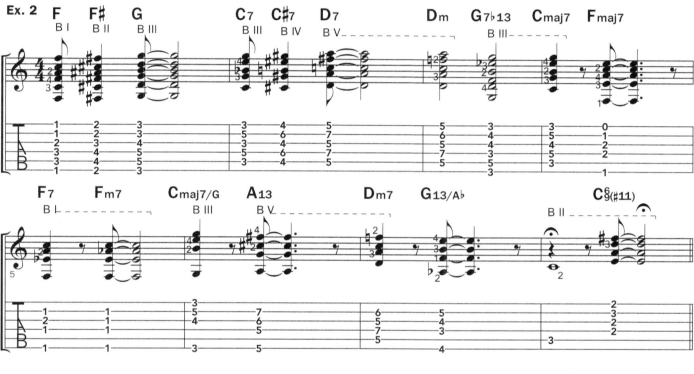

A partial barre with the top strings uncovered.

A partial barre with the lower strings uncovered.

THE ALEX DE GRASSI FINGERSTYLE GUITAR METHOD

(two strings), 3/6 (three strings), 2/3 or 4/6 (four strings), and 5/6 (five strings). The strings to be barred are deduced from the music and tab.

Partial barres make it possible to combine fretted and open strings, providing textural contrast and allowing for some new chord voicings. In **Example 3**, the open strings give the fretting hand time to make smooth position changes and allow the notes of the arpeggio to flow into each other. Note that in measure 3 the fourth finger frets the string (the third string) positioned between the barred and nonbarred strings, allowing the partial barre to be executed cleanly. Due to the angling of the barring finger, there is usually a "transition" string that needs to either be fretted, avoided, or muted, because it is difficult to play the open string cleanly.

Playing the open string cleanly is not an issue with the second type of partial barre chords, in which the barring finger simply extends flat across the required number of strings, leaving lower strings untouched. This type of barre is useful for accessing bass notes on an open strings while playing chords in higher positions, as in measures 7, 8, and 15. Note that in measures 7 and 8 the partial barre can be applied and released for just three notes while the third and fourth fingers can be held throughout the two-measure ascending/descending arpeggio. The partial barre is less restrictive and allows more flexibility than the full barre. In measures 13 and 14, the barre is placed across strings 5, 4, and 3. Both the sixth and the first strings are left open. This type of "inside" partial barre requires that the fingertip joint bend back slightly.

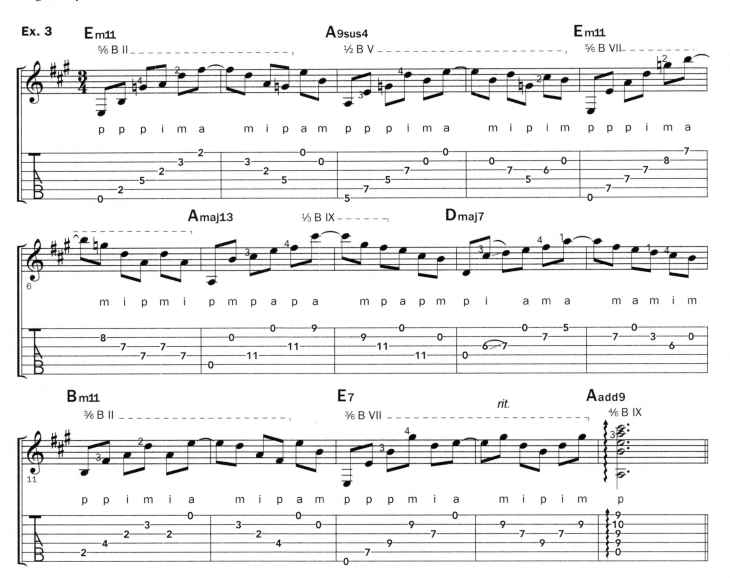

Cross-String Arpeggios and Chords

The phrasing, voicing, and range of arpeggios can be altered and extended when played cross-string. The technique also allows arpeggios to be easily and fluidly integrated with melodic lines. As with first- and second-position chords, the notes of cross-string arpeggios are typically allowed to ring beyond their written values until the chord changes, unless otherwise specified in the score.

The arpeggios in **Example 4a** use some standard seventh-chord voicings, but they have a different, perhaps smoother phrasing than their counterparts lower on the fingerboard. They don't require hammer-ons or pull-offs, and they never play consecutive notes on the same string, giving them a harp-like quality (keep in mind the origin of the word *arpeggiare*—to play like a harp). This also makes them easier to play, though it may take awhile to get used to the new fingerings. Play the passage, then compare the sound and feel with the same arpeggios played in first and second positions in **Example 4b**.

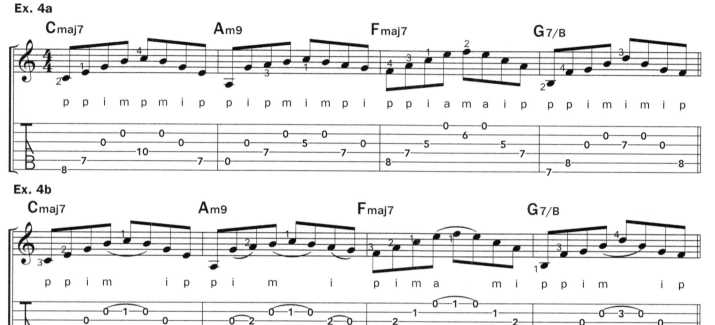

Both the range and length of the arpeggios can be extended using fretting-hand position shifts as shown in **Example 5**. The A7 arpeggio extends over two measures and includes the interval of the ninth (B) for added color. By use of a couple of hammer-ons and a pull-off, the following Em, F, and G7 arpeggios are extended. (The Em has a range of three octaves and extends over three measures.) However, the first note (the root) of each of these four chords cannot be held for the entire length of the arpeggio. Strive for a smooth flow from the beginning to the end of each arpeggio.

Introducing some new intervals and nonsequential notes can give arpeggios a more melodic sound. In **Example 6a**, the arpeggios outline chords, but in a less obvious way.

120 THE ALEX DE GRASSI FINGERSTYLE GUITAR METHOD

MOVING UP THE FINGERBOARD
Cross-String Arpeggios

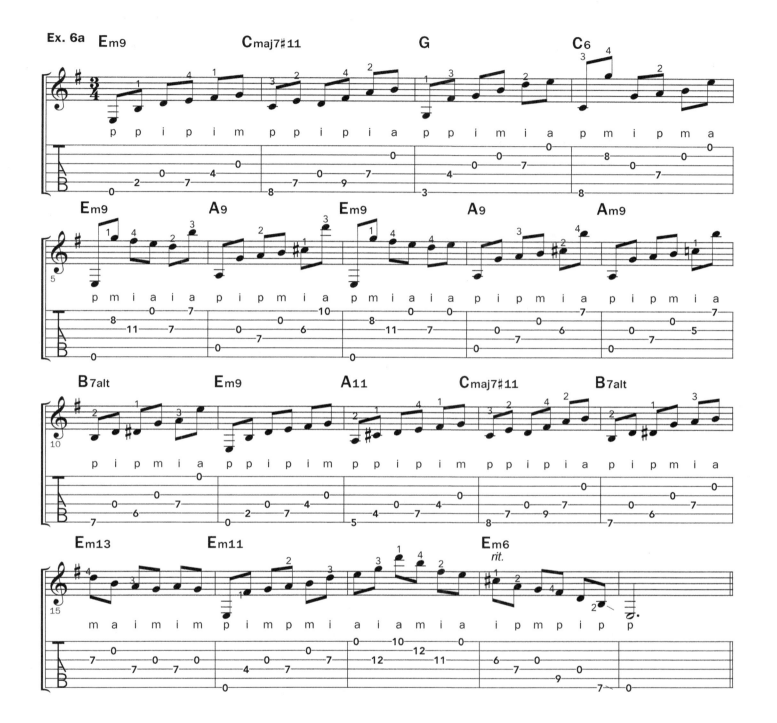

By playing with note values, accents, and articulations, a melody can be extracted and the accompaniment can be arranged to produce the finished composition shown in **Example 6b**. The arpeggio is now broken into three separate voices: the melody (up-stem notes), the long bass notes (down-stem), and the inner voice accompaniment that fills out the arpeggios (down-stem notes). Accent the melody and play the accompaniment notes lightly. Be sure to let the bass notes sustain for their full value. Notice that some notes have both up stems and down stems. This is to indicate that they function as both melody notes and accompaniment. The E on the upbeat of measure 4 functions as both an eighth note in the melody and as a half note in the accompaniment. Let it ring as you continue with the melody.

MOVING UP THE FINGERBOARD
Cross-String Arpeggios

Cross-string technique can be integrated with full barre chords to good effect. The triplet runs of the blues shuffle in **Example 7** are given a distinct textural quality when played cross-string, leaving the fretting hand free to deliver articulations like slides and bends as marked in the score. Then in measure 5, the barre facilitates playing the alternating bass together with the melody notes occurring at the seventh fret. There in the final measure, the barre makes it possible to hold the bass note through the measure while playing the block chords against it.

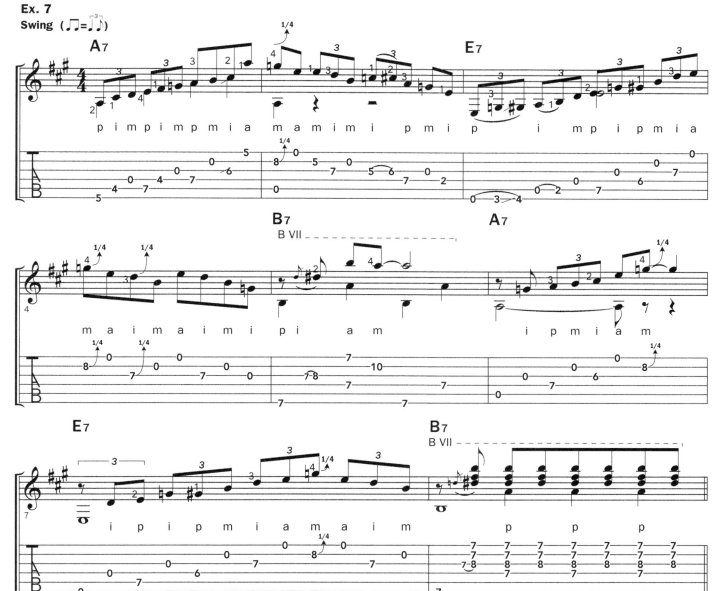

Section 8
Alternate Tunings

Voicings, Resonance, Modes,
and Harmony 126

Texture and Weight 132

Audio Playlist 2, Tracks 23–43

Throughout the development of the guitar and its predecessors, players have experimented with tunings. In the classical repertoire, it's not uncommon to find music composed using dropped-D tuning (with the sixth string lowered to D) or even the tuning D G D G B E (with both the sixth and fifth strings lowered a whole step). Steel-string guitars are particularly adaptable to alternate or "open" tunings, because the higher tension allows for a wider variation in the tuning. Some popular alternate tunings like open D or open G were originally developed for specialized guitars like the dobro or lap guitar, and also for the banjo. In the past 30 or 40 years, many new (and some very unusual) alternate tunings have evolved, and today their use is common among fingerstyle players. Tunings like D A D G A D are widely used, while others are rather esoteric and unique to a particular player. There are many reasons to use alternate tunings: access to open strings, new chord voicings, juxtaposition of certain groups of notes, sonic textures, and increased resonance among them. An alternate tuning might also be useful for playing in a particular key, or extending the range of the instrument. In any case, retuning the guitar provides an opportunity to explore and make new discoveries, and perhaps a chance to escape the conventions of what we already know. This section will explore some different tunings and consider some of the advantages they have to offer.

Voicings, Resonance, Modes, and Harmony

The way a guitar is tuned can seriously alter our perception of what is harmonically possible on the instrument. The relationship between the pitches of both the open strings and fretted notes changes with the tuning. For example, certain chords and key signatures in standard tuning can take advantage of open strings, most notably E, E minor, A, A minor, G, C, D, and D minor. You can use one or more open strings to play in any of these keys. However, the open strings of many alternate tunings spell out a chord or mode. This tends to reinforce certain overtones and can actually make the guitar sound louder and more resonant. It also makes the tuning well suited to cross-string picking in certain keys, allowing for contrasting textures between open and fretted strings. The rearranged juxtaposition of intervals also opens the door to a variety of chord voicings and combinations of notes not possible in standard tuning.

Dropped D

Perhaps the simplest and most common alternate tuning is dropped D, where the sixth string is tuned down to D. This extends the range by a whole step and, in the key of D, makes it easy to play the root (tonic) no matter what position the fretting hand plays. Strum the chords in **Example 1** and listen to the resonance. In the first chord there are D notes in three different octaves as well as two A notes and one F♯. The repetition of the intervals of tonic and fifth reinforces the resonance of those pitches and their overtones, often making the guitar sound louder. The second chord removes the F♯ and adds an A on top so that all the pitches are either the tonic or the fifth. (This might even sound louder.) Play through the other voicings and listen for the full resonance.

In **Example 2** a chord melody is played over a *pedaled bass*. The pedaled bass is simply a repeated note, sometimes referred to as a drone bass. In the seventh measure, the bass begins to move with the chords to bring the pedal to a cadence. The ending is tagged with a little blues lick.

Tempered vs. Just Intonation

Since Bach's time, pianos have been tuned to equal temperament, wherein the true mathematical relationship of overtones is slightly altered to make the intervals sound equal in all keys. The guitar is typically tuned using equal temperament for the same reasons; however it is possible, depending on the guitar and the tuning, to achieve a more "just" (more mathematically correct) intonation on the open strings of the guitar. This may contribute to reinforcement of certain overtones, especially those of the third, fifth, and octave intervals, that increase resonance of the instrument. The difference is often most noticeable when playing a chord comprised of harmonics or open strings. A more just intonation may, however, also make it difficult to modulate to certain keys and still sound in tune. With some effort, you can compensate the pitches of fretted notes by "pushing" or "pulling" particular notes sharp or flat, but, especially with fast or difficult pieces, this can be difficult or impossible. As you experiment with tunings, be aware of these minor anomalies and be prepared to make minor adjustments to both the tuning and the way you fret particular notes.

Tuning Tracks

- Dropped D
- Open D
- D A D G A D
- C G D G A D
- D A D E A D
- D A D G C F
- E♭ G D G B♭ D
- D A D F G C
- D A D G C E♭

ALTERNATE TUNINGS
Voicings, Resonance, Modes, and Harmony

Ex. 1
Dropped-D Tuning: D A D G B E

Ex. 2
Dropped-D Tuning: D A D G B E

Other Tunings

When the tuning of a string is altered, notes on that string are now available in different positions on the fingerboard. Tunings like open D (from low to high, D A D F# A D) and open G (D G D G B D) are tuned to major chords. These tunings make it easy to play modally (see the sidebar "Modes") by picking out single lines and mixing modes against a background drone of the tonic (D) and fifth (A), as illustrated in **Example 3**. The mode can easily change from major to minor, as is does in measure 2, or any other mode that has the notes D and A in it simply by changing the mode played on the third and fourth strings. The drone notes played on strings 1, 2, 5, and 6 are allowed to ring throughout the example.

It's also easy to play I–IV–V and other common progressions in these tunings simply by barring across the strings with a single finger. **Example 4** shows a typical folk picking pattern in open D

Ex. 3
Open-D Tuning: D A D F# A D

Modes

In Western harmony, the major scale contains seven modes—each with Greek names. Each mode begins and ends on a different degree of the scale. The major scale is called Ionian and begins on the tonic. The second mode is a minor called Dorian and begins on the second degree of the scale. The third, or Phrygian, mode is also a minor, and begins on the third degree of the scale, and so on (see table below). It's possible to play in one or more of these modes without leaving the major scale. For example, one can play in a D Mixolydian mode (starting on the fifth degree of the G scale) in a D tuning but stay in the key of G. This is quite common in folk music. There are many other modes besides these seven found in music from around the world.

Major-Scale Modes

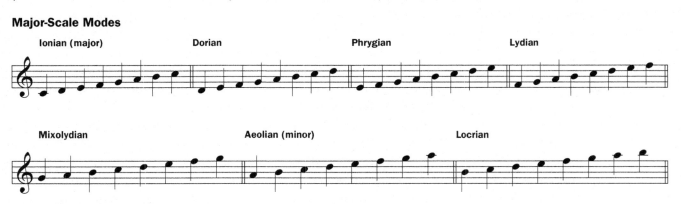

ALTERNATE TUNINGS
Voicings, Resonance, Modes, and Harmony

playing a I–IV–I–II–V–I chord progression using barres. (Unless otherwise noted, use *p* on strings 6–4, and *i, m,* and *a* on strings 3, 2, and 1, respectively.) Note that the voices all move together in parallel motion. That works well for some types of music, but it has harmonic limitations. Using more complex fretting-hand positions, a variety of chord voicings can also be formed in open D and G tunings, but the potential seems to be somewhat limited compared to both standard tuning and other kinds of alternate tunings.

Tunings that have intervals of a second between strings, like D A D G A D or D A D E A D, seem to offer greater harmonic potential. They make possible some close or "tight" (pitches close

Ex. 4
Open-D Tuning: D A D F♯ A D

TRACK 35

THE ALEX DE GRASSI FINGERSTYLE GUITAR METHOD

together) voicings that are difficult to find in standard tuning. For example, the jazz piano voicings 1–7–9–3–5, 1–3–5–6–9, 1–3–6–7–9, or 1–3–4–5 are difficult to reach in standard or D tuning, but more readily achieved in D A D G A D, as shown in **Example 5**.

However, in D A D G A D, the roots of those voicings are hard to reach in most keys. It works when the root is an open string like D or A, but not as well when the root requires a fretted note. The related tuning C G D G A D makes chords like these movable from one position to another—the interval of a ninth between the

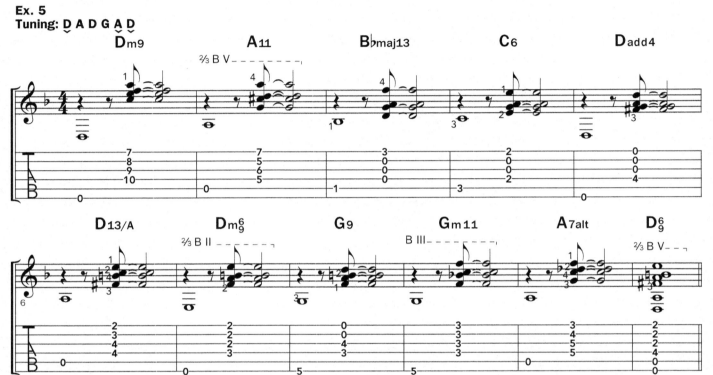

Chord Naming

Chord names vary depending on the musical context. Take, for instance, the Dm9 in measure 1 of Example 5. In a jazz context it's understood that the Dm9 would have a dominant 7th (C) in it, though it's not included in the name. The same for the Gm11 and G9 chords. The D13/A and the Dm6/9 (or G7/D) in measures 6 and 7 are a little unusual, so both 6 and 9 are included to better define them. The D6/9 is a major chord, and is often simply written as D or Dmaj7. In a different context, these chords might be renamed or have all the intervals beyond the triad (1, 3, 5) spelled out even if the pitches are identical to those shown here.

ALTERNATE TUNINGS
Voicings, Resonance, Modes, and Harmony

sixth and fourth strings makes it easy to have the root in the bass and build the rest of the chord beginning on the third or the seventh. This makes it possible to modulate and play in different keys as demonstrated in the jazz waltz in **Example 6**. Note that most of these chords do not repeat the root—they are five-note voicings. The dominant seventh chords like F7 in measure 2 may have the sixth and ninth in them as well. All the chords in this example are typical jazz piano voicings. (Tip: When tuning the fifth and sixth strings down to G and C, it may be necessary to use a heavier gauge string in order to maintain a good tone and keep the string from buzzing.)

Ex. 6
Tuning: C G D G A D

Texture and Weight

Altering the tuning changes both the overall string tension on the guitar and the tension of individual strings. Raised string tension can make for a faster attack and a brighter sound. Lowered tension can facilitate bends and pitch modulation, slow the attack, and yield a darker sound. Some tunings facilitate doubling or tripling of pitches to create unisons that lend weight to a chord or single note. In conjunction with the "altered resonance" particular to the tuning, a unique sonic texture can be achieved.

Let's begin with unisons. Pitches doubled or even tripled on adjacent strings can be used to set up rhythmic patterns with contrasting textures. **Example 1** is an excerpt from "Turning: Turning Back" that uses the tuning D A D E A D. The fretting hand holds a position so that strings 2, 3, and 4 are all in unison on A. The fifth string is played open as an A an octave below. Each string can be articulated differently, just like a drummer striking different parts of the drumhead to create a textured pattern.

In this example, the open second string provides a drone texture and is allowed to sustain longer than the others. The third string is played with the first fretting-hand finger almost on top of the fret, quickly letting up after each note for a slightly muted, staccato effect. The note duration of the A on the fourth string can be controlled—it's generally held more like an eighth note with the third fretting-hand finger applying a small amount of pitch modulation. The fifth string provides a low sound. The resulting effect is analogous to a percussion pattern: the edge of the drumhead gives the dry, staccato sound (third string), midway between the center and edge of the drum gives a fuller, more sustained sound (fourth string), and the center of the drum gives the long, low sustained note (fifth string). In addition to its function as a rhythmic drone, the second string (along with the third) is also sometimes used to play melody notes.

Once the pattern is established in measures 1 and 2, a melody can be interwoven with the drumming pattern. Even though

ALTERNATE TUNINGS
Texture and Weight

Ex. 1: "Turning: Turning Back"
Tuning: D A D E A D

the pattern is momentarily broken, the ear continues to fill it in, with a little help from the rhythm of the melodic line.

Unisons also can lend weight or added texture to a phrase. In my arrangement of the traditional folk song "Single Girl" (**Example 2**) in C G D G A D tuning, the first two notes of the melody in measure 1, 3, and 5 are doubled up. This adds some heft and gives that part of the phrase a chorus effect, like two or more people singing the same note. One of the doubled notes on beat one of measure 1 has a grace-note slur from a half tone below. This accentuates the chorus effect by approximating the sound of two voices singing in unison but slightly out of sync. The last chord in the example has unison C's on the top note and a C played an octave below. That's a lot of weight (three Cs!) used for emphasis of the IV chord cadence. Note also the tight (close) chord voicings in the last two measures preceding the cadence.

Ex. 2: "Single Girl"
Tuning: C G D G A D

ALTERNATE TUNINGS
Texture and Weight

Tunings and String Tension

The raised or lowered tension of open tunings can alter the sonic texture of the guitar. The lower tension of the C G D G A D tuning makes it easier to use pitch modulation. It's also possible to get a little of the "spreading" sound characteristic of a fretless bass. **Example 3**, an excerpt from my composition "The Water Garden," uses both these articulations throughout the piece to convey the image of floating on water (note the marking "like the surface of water"). The pliability of the strings is well suited to the mood of the piece. However, one should take care with the intonation when using low-tension tunings because the pitch of fretted notes is more easily modulated, particularly on the fifth and sixth strings. It may be necessary to slightly pull or push the fretting finger to adjust the intonation, especially in the higher positions. Note that the tuning makes some interesting inversions possible in the last few measures.

Ex. 3: "The Water Garden"
Tuning: C G D G A D

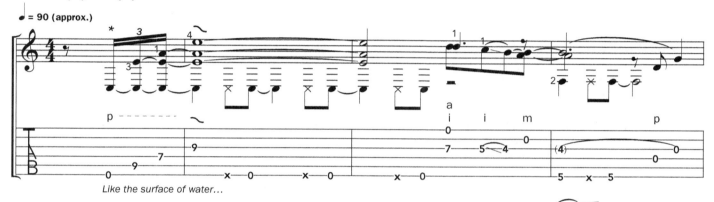

Like the surface of water...

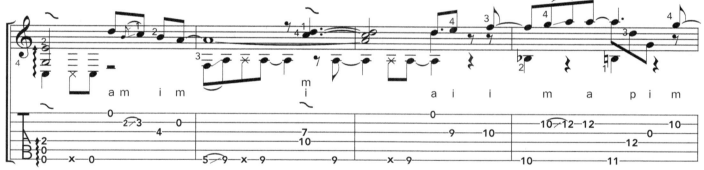

metalico

* The 16th-note triplets in the pickup measure indicate a very slow strum landing on the third string (E) on the downbeat. This notation is used when a strum is sufficiently drawn out.

THE ALEX DE GRASSI FINGERSTYLE GUITAR METHOD

Increasing the string tension can produce a brighter texture with a faster attack. The tuning D A D G C F, used to play my British Isles–inspired piece "McCormick" (**Example 4**), lowers the sixth string but raises the first and second strings, expanding the range by a minor third. The sixth string is somewhat more relaxed, but the overall tension is greater—especially on the top two strings—making the tuning suitable for the bright, crisp attack needed to execute the many hammer-ons and pull-offs played at a fast tempo. Though the strings are slightly more rigid, they require less "travel" and respond more immediately to the small, quick bends that occur in measures 6 and 8.

Note that the piece is played in the keys of F and B♭ though the bass is tuned to D. The open low D string is used for passages played in D minor—the relative minor of F. The melody is played cross-string using the open first and second strings together with higher position fretted notes. Note how the melody note C is doubled on beat two-*and* of measures 14, 16, and 18 to give it some weight. The fretted note is given vibrato to create contrast and tension with the sound of the open string. Notes in parentheses, like the G in measures 6 and 8, should be barely audible. They function as rhythm notes and shouldn't be considered part of any line.

ALTERNATE TUNINGS
Texture and Weight

*Vibrato for fourth string only.

Tunings and Keys

Many altered tunings use "white key" pitches (no flats or sharps) for the open strings, encouraging the keys with sharps or no accidentals. A lot of jazz and blues is played in the flat keys often preferred by horn players. The following excerpt from my arrangement of the blues classic "St. James Infirmary" (**Example 5**) is played in G minor—the relative minor of B♭—using the tuning E♭ G D G B♭ D. The relaxed tension is conducive to articulations like pitch modulation, vibrato, and slides. Note that many of the longer notes (half notes and dotted halves) are marked vibrato, while shorter held notes (eighth and quarters) are marked pitch modulation. A slow, rising pitch works well for many of the shorter notes, but experiment with speed and depth with each note. Vary the speed of the slides as well.

Ex. 5: "St. James Infirmary"
Tuning: E♭ G D G B♭ D

ALTERNATE TUNINGS
Texture and Weight

In E♭ G D G B♭ D tuning, the relationships of a major third between the sixth and fifth strings, and between the second and first strings, as well as the minor third relationship between the third and second strings, make for some interesting chord voicings and juxtaposition of notes. In general, the tuning is well adapted to a more complex harmonic palette while making good use of open strings. This frees the fretting hand to execute some highly ornamented lines consisting of hammer-ons, pull-offs, and cross-string fingerings. These rapid, intricate lines contrast nicely with all the vibratos, pitch modulations, and slides and with the overall slow tempo of the piece.

The Example 5 arrangement is played in the key of G minor, which is spelled out by the open strings 5–1, but it's also a natural for playing in B♭ major, E♭ major, and C minor. **Example 6** is an excerpt from my arrangement of "Shortnin' Bread" in B♭. This up-tempo piece has a simpler harmonic structure, but the tuning works well for weaving together intricate chromatic lines using cross-string techniques. The theme is stated in measures 1–8 as two voices: melody and bass. The notes of both lines should be crisp and kept to their written values by applying and releasing the barre with the first finger. Use *p* to stop the bass notes where necessary.

Measures 9 through the end of the excerpt are played cross-string. In measures 9–12, the bass line becomes more defined (stems down) by accenting the notes and holding them to their written value. This will allow the notes of the upper voice (which are played more softly) to speak through. The tempo makes it hard to stop open strings of the upper voice (though it can be done), but they will have a shorter apparent duration if they are played with less volume than the notes of the bass line.

The remainder of the excerpt is mostly a single voice with a few held notes in a second voice. Experiment with controlling note durations of both open and fretted notes. With more control the lines will have a tighter, more defined texture, and where notes are allowed to ring they will have a more legato, free-flowing texture. Hold bass notes to their durations in the last line. They function to bring the passage to a cadence before returning to the top at the repeat.

Ex. 6: "Shortnin' Bread"
Tuning: E♭ G D G B♭ D

* Tied on repeat

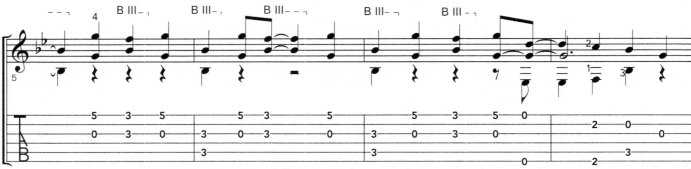

ALTERNATE TUNINGS
Texture and Weight

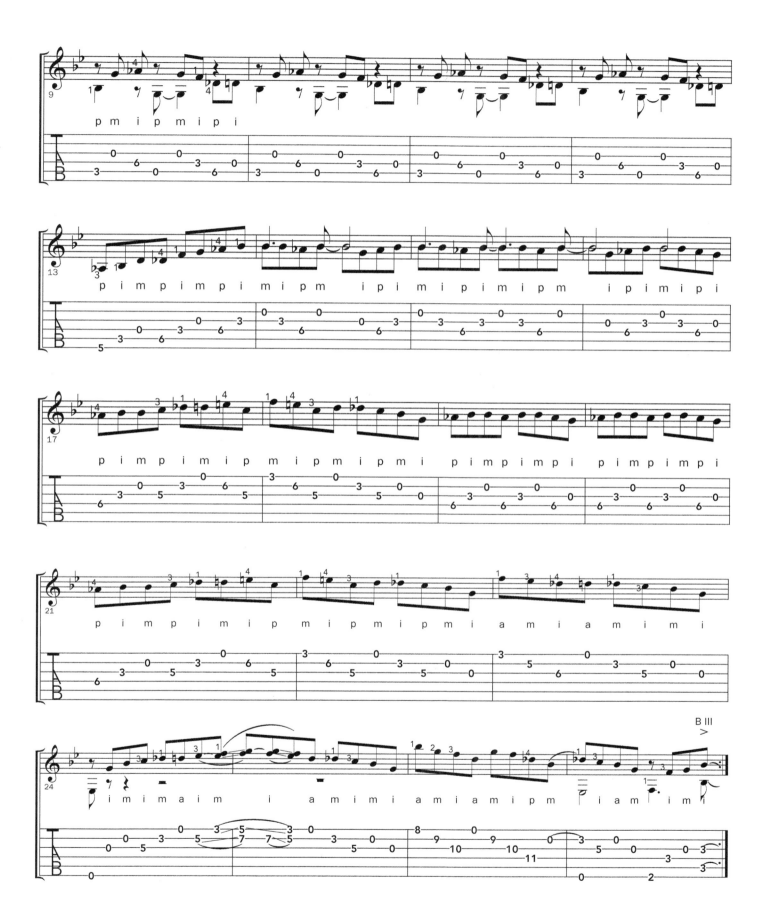

Section 9
About Time

Cross-Rhythms 144

Arpeggiated Figures 150

Phrasing 158

Audio Playlist 2, Tracks 44–66

The polyphonic nature of fingerstyle guitar makes it possible to play lines like melody, countermelody, and bass simultaneously as independent voices. Not only can these voices have different pitches, articulations, and dynamics, but they can each have their own phrasing or even suggest separate rhythms and meters. Developing independence between the thumb and fingers of the picking hand is key to making this work. This section will look at how cross-rhythms (or polyrhythms), arpeggiated figures, and independent phrasing of voices can be integrated to add dimension to a fingerstyle arrangement.

Cross-Rhythms

Fingerstyle technique is well suited to playing *cross-rhythms*—more than one meter simultaneously. For example, a 3/4 meter is typically divided into three beats (triple meter), with the quarter note (♩) getting the beat. It can also be divided into two beats (duple meter) with the dotted quarter (♩.) getting the beat. Set the metronome at a medium 3/4 tempo (120 bpm) and tap along with your foot while counting "*one*-and *two*-and *three*-and." Keep tapping your foot with the metronome, and begin tapping your opposite hand against your leg or a table on the one and the *and* of two while counting "*one*-and *two-and three*-and." The foot is grouping the six eighth notes into three groups of two while the hand is grouping the eighth notes into two groups of three as shown in **Example 1a**. Continue tapping the foot and hand but start counting the hand taps as "one two." This is the basic two-against-three cross-rhythm shown in **Example 1b**.

Reverse the roles—so your hand is tapping quarter notes with the metronome, and your foot is tapping dotted quarters. Count first with the hand in three, then count the cross-rhythm with your foot as shown in **Examples 1c and 1d**. For most people, whatever the foot is doing will seem like the main rhythm and the hand will feel like the cross-rhythm, so this is more difficult.

Now set the metronome to ♩ = 80 bpm and tap your foot along while counting *one*, *two* in 2/4 time, as shown in **Example 1e**. The hand is tapping the cross-rhythm as a series of quarter-note triplets. (Each triplet has the same time value as the quarter notes played at 120 bpm in Example 1a.) It may be easier to feel the three triples when only counting the one of each measure of 2/4. Try that before counting the triplets and tapping two beats per measure with the foot in **Example 1f**. Reverse the roles of hand and foot so the hand is now tapping quarter notes along with the metronome. Count the quarter-note beats in **Example 1g** and then the quarter-note triplet cross-rhythm as shown in **Example 1h**.

In **Example 2a**, the figure in the top line is counted in 3/4 while the figure in the bottom line is felt as 2/4 or 6/8. Count three beats (*one*-and *two*-and *three*-and) per measure and play the top line on the beat. Play the dotted quarters of the lower voice on the one and the *and* of two. Once that feels comfortable, play **Example 2b**. It's the same phrase, rewritten in 2/4. Count

ABOUT TIME
Cross-Rhythms

two beats per measure in 2/4 while playing quarter-note triplets in the top line. The same phrase is written in 6/8 in **Example 2c.** Now the bottom line is on the beat (*one* two three, *two* two three), and the top line plays the cross-rhythm (*one* two *three*, two *two* three). Use *p* for the lower line (stems down) and a combination of *i, m,* and *a* for the upper line. The opposition of thumb and fingers makes it easier to feel the two separate rhythms.

Try to keep the speed constant as you play the different time signatures. All the measures should occupy the same space of time. Note that the tempo marking is 120 for Example 2a and 80 for 2b and 2c—the same 3:2 ratio (120/80 equals 3/2) of the cross-rhythms. The 6/8 and 2/4 interpretations are played at a tempo that is 2/3 the speed of the 3/4 time signature. With practice, you'll begin to feel both rhythms simultaneously.

Try the longer phrase in **Example 3**. Note that in measures 7 and 8 some notes are tied over to vary the rhythmic structure as it approaches the cadence. Using Example 2 as a guide, try playing Example 3 at the same speed but counting it in 3/4, then in 2/4, and then in 6/8. Mathematically all three time signatures are the same thing, but the meter and the implied cultural tradition behind it might suggest a slightly different feel. Experiment with the feel and the tempo to bring out different rhythms like waltz (3/4), cut-time march (2/4), and jig (6/8).

Cross-rhythms have a multidimensional feel that creates dynamic tension. The two rhythms seem to pull the listener (and the player) in two directions simultaneously. Cross-rhythms can be used continuously in a piece, but they are often used more sparingly. They can be introduced to add tension to a phrase, then removed to resolve tension. In my D A D G A D arrangement

Ex. 3

THE ALEX DE GRASSI FINGERSTYLE GUITAR METHOD

of the French lullaby "Fais Do-Do," shown in **Example 4**, the underlying rhythmic structure is a three-against-two cross-rhythm. The melody is clearly in 3/4, and the lower voice (stems down) has a dotted-quarter pulse that provides a 2/4 cross-rhythm. The cross-rhythm is established in the first two measures, then relaxes to a straight 3/4 feel in measures 3 and 4. The cross-rhythm returns in measures 5 and 6, relaxes in measure 7, and then returns in measure 8. A more final resolution is achieved with the half-note, quarter-note, dotted-half-note bass line in the final two measures of the second ending. Use *p* for all the down-stem notes.

ABOUT TIME
Cross-Rhythms

A four-against-three cross-rhythm can be achieved by further subdividing note values. If the dotted quarter notes of the lower voice are halved, they become dotted eighth notes. The lower voice of **Example 5a** is counted "*one*-ee-and-*a* two-ee-*and*-a *three*-ee-and-a." The top line is counted "*one*-and *two*-and *three*-and." Use *p* for the lower voice and *a* and *m* for the first two strings.

In **Example 5b** the phrase has been rewritten in 12/16 so the dotted eighth notes of the lower line get the beat. Now the bottom line is counted "*one* two three, *two* two three, *three* two three, *four* two three," and the top line is counted "*one* two *three*, two *two* three, *three* two *three*, four *two* three." The time signature 12/16 would typically indicate a faster tempo, so in **Example 5c** the phrase has been written in the more commonly used 12/8. In **Example 5d**, the phrase has been rewritten in 4/4.

The bottom line is counted "one two three four" while the top line is counted as quarter-note triplets (*one* two three, *two* two three).

This strategy of subdividing the beat is used later in the piece "Fais Do-Do," as shown in **Example 6**. The dotted quarter notes of the lower voice are halved to produce four dotted eighth notes per measure. Sometimes they are combined with dotted quarters, but the intention of the dotted-eighth cross-rhythm is still there. Remember, cross-rhythms are a tool, and the patterns of the exercises are meant to enhance rather than replace musical lines. Counting 16th notes, the combined notes of both voices in measure 1 would be counted as follows:

1   2   3   -   and

1 - ee - and - **a**   2 - ee - **and** - a   3 - ee - and - a

Once the math has been worked out, some people find it easier to count and/or read four (quarter-note quartuplets) against three without having to count and/or read all the 16th notes. The bottom line of the passage could also be written as a series of quarter-note quartuplets, as shown in **Example 7.**

Cross-rhythms can provide a means for development of an arrangement. In **Example 8,** a three-against-two cross-rhythm is the basis for a short, transitional interlude that serves to modulate from the G-minor to the C-minor statements of the theme in my arrangement of "St. James Infirmary." The introduction of the cross-rhythm breaks up the rhythmic feel of the piece and provides a contrasting section.

Ex. 7
Tuning: D A D G A D

ABOUT TIME
Cross-Rhythms

Ex. 8: "St. James Infirmary"
Tuning: E♭ G D G B♭ D

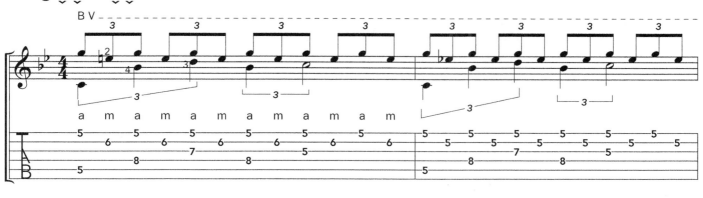
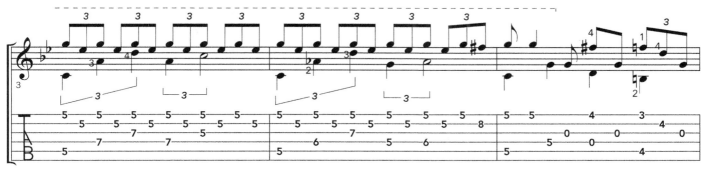
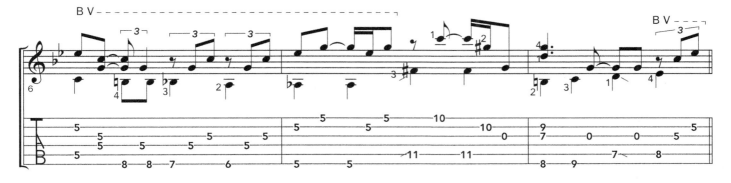

Arpeggiated Figures, Syncopations, and Accents

Arpeggios can be used to group notes into myriad rhythmic patterns and figures. A figure is a short repeating series of notes that can be identified by the pattern of the pitches and/or the pattern of the note values. The eighth notes in **Example 1** are grouped in a three-three-two pattern to form a syncopated rhythm counted "*one*-and two-*and* three-and *four*-and." The up-stem notes form voice 1—they are all eighth notes. The down-stem notes form a second voice that plays a dotted-quarter, dotted-quarter, quarter figure. The down-stem notes also double as the first up-stem eighth note of each voice 1 grouping. By accenting voice 2 notes and holding them to their written values, the line stands out clearly and outlines a syncopated rhythm.

The motif has been rewritten and extended in **Example 2**. The lower voice has been split into two voices to form a third voice comprised of whole notes on the downbeat of each measure. The whole notes (voice 3) can also function as part of the dotted-quarter, dotted-quarter, quarter pattern of the second voice. This depends on how accents are placed, and on variations in timbre and articulation. If the voice 2 and voice 3 notes are given similar volume, timbre, and articulation, the whole notes seem to function in both voices. If voice 3 notes are played at a different volume, and/or the voice 2 notes are articulated differently (played *metalico*, for example, and/or given slight pitch modulation), the two voices sound more distinct. Experiment with these variables. Then try to hear all three voices simultaneously as one part, and as distinct parts.

The 16th notes in **Example 3** have been grouped into a three-three-three-three-two-two pattern to give a highly syncopated dotted-eighth, dotted-eighth, dotted-eighth, dotted-eighth, eighth, eighth figure in the lower voice. Note that the first four notes in the lower voice form a four-against-three cross-rhythm with the first three groups of eighth notes in the upper voice. The fourth beat in the measure breaks the cross-rhythm. The overall effect is jagged and asymmetrical. Use *p* for all the down-stem notes and *a* and *m* for the first and second strings throughout.

Ex. 1

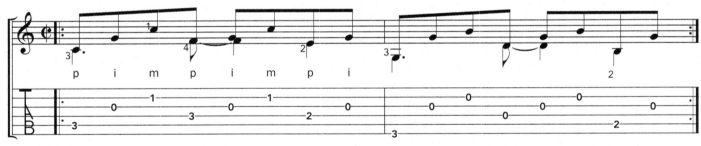

ABOUT TIME
Arpeggiated Figures, Syncopations, and Accents

Ex. 2

Ex. 3

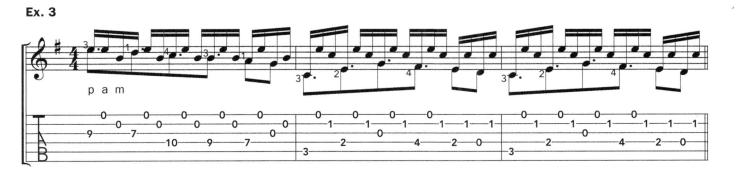

A cross-rhythm can be introduced into an arpeggio momentarily by changing the figure in the lower voice and altering the pattern of the arpeggio. **Example 4** shows a simple four-note arpeggio pattern, in which the lowest note plays a bass figure comprising three quarter notes. When changed to a three-note arpeggio pattern, the bass figure becomes four dotted eighth notes, creating a four-against-three cross-rhythm. This gives the illusion that the time is compressed, speeding up momentarily, even though the tempo remains the same.

A compression effect can be achieved by inserting additional notes between beats. In **Example 5a**, the 3/4 arpeggio comprises all eighth notes, with a quarter-note figure in the lower voice. Without changing the tempo or note durations of the lower voice, an extra note is inserted into each beat in **Example 5b** so that the upper voice becomes eighth-note triplets. In **Example 5c**, another note is inserted between beats to form a 16th-note arpeggio.

Another note is added to make quintuplets in the upper voice in **Example 5d**. Finally, one more 16th note is inserted in **Example 5e** to form 16th-note sextuplets (or pairs of 16th-note triplets).

The progression from Example 5a to 5e thickens the texture of the arpeggio while maintaining the underlying 3/4 rhythm. As the density increases, move the picking hand closer to the bridge to give better definition to the arpeggios.

Another way to compress an arpeggio is by redistributing or shifting the note values slightly to straighten out a line. In **Example 6**, the three-three-two arpeggio is transformed into a smoother three-three-three grouping by converting the dotted-eighth, dotted-eighth, eighth pattern in the lower voice to three quarter-note triplets and inserting a 16th note into the upper voice. The tempo and the meter remain the same, but the eighth notes occur slightly faster—closer together. Each group of three 16th notes has the same value as a quarter note triplet.

Ex. 4

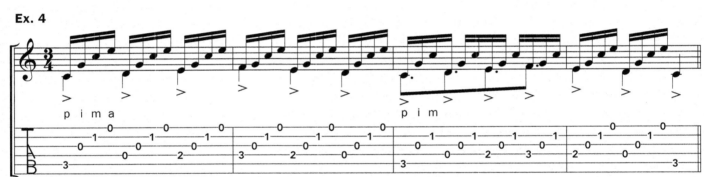

ABOUT TIME
Arpeggiated Figures, Syncopations, and Accents

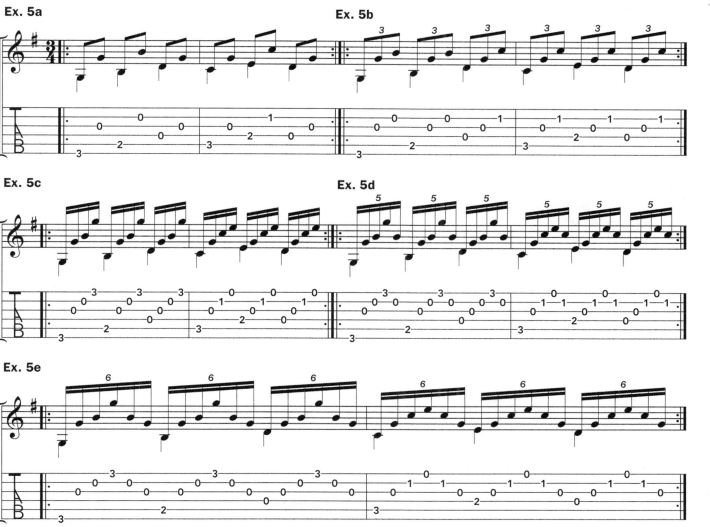

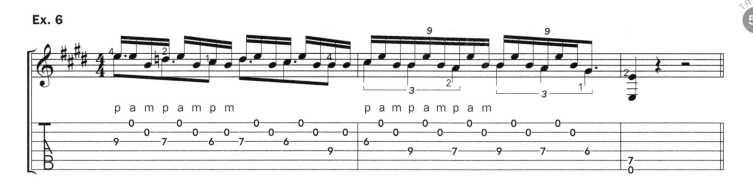

Both cross-rhythms and the compressing/expanding effect can be used as a way to transition from one meter to another, as demonstrated in **Example 7**. Set the metronome to somewhere between 100 and 120 bpm and tap your foot in cut time on the half note (every other beat) throughout the example. The example begins with the same first two measures of Example 6. Then, without changing the tempo, the half note beat of the first two measures becomes the dotted-half beat of the 6/8 time signature in measure 3. In measure 6, the quarter-note syncopation becomes the quarter-note beat as the meter transitions to 3/4 time in measure 7. The 3/4 section is sufficiently fast that one only needs to count the downbeat, or dotted half note, which is still the same value (every other beat) as the dotted half in measures 3–6. (When each quarter note is counted, the metronome will sound like it is playing a two-against-three cross-rhythm.) The length of that downbeat is equivalent to the dotted half of the returning 6/8 section beginning in measure 11. Finally, the dotted half of the 6/8 section is equivalent to the half note as the

piece returns (D.C.) to the beginning of the piece in 4/4. The rhythms change, the beats are regrouped, and the figures change. However, the example can be played as a continuous, seamless loop tapping every other beat without resetting the metronome or breaking the flow of the pulse.

Accents

How, or even if, cross-rhythms are perceived can depend on the use of accents, as well as the use of repeating figures. **Example 8a** shows a simple 12/8 arpeggio. The *p* strokes outline the accented dotted quarter notes of each beat, and the fingers play the remaining eighth notes. In **Example 8b**, the arpeggio is altered so that the thumb is playing every other note. Though it sounds somewhat syncopated, by keeping the accents on the first note of each eighth-note triplet, you can retain the 12/8 feel and continue to count the phrase "*one* two three, *two* two three, *three* two three, *four* two three."

However, when the same arpeggio is played with the accents placed on all the thumb strokes (every other note), as in **Example 8c**, a 6/4 cross-rhythm with a six-note figure (C–E–G–F–A–G) emerges. First count "*one* two *three*, two two three, *three* two three, four *two* three" while continuing to tap your foot in four (on the first beat of each eighth-note triplet group). Then tap your foot on all the accented notes as shown in measure 2 of Example 8c. Now the beat is on the quarter note and the lower line is counted "*one*-and *two*-and *three*-and *four*-and *five*-and *six*-and," with a 6/4 time signature. The two lines together look like this:

12/8 **1** 2 3, **2** 2 3, **3** 2 3, **4** 2 3

6/4 **1** - and **2** - and **3** - and **4** - and **5** - and **6** - and

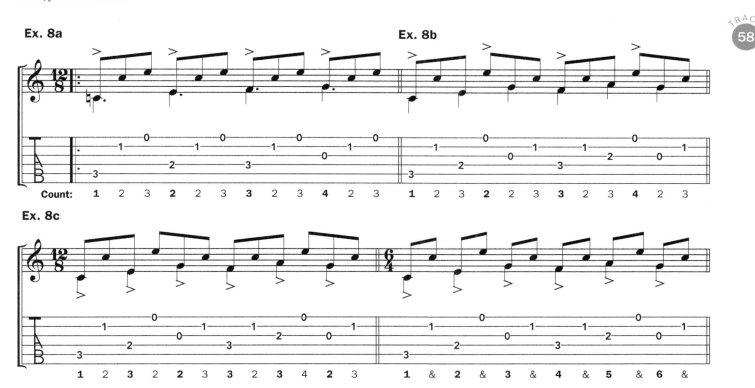

In **Example 8d**, the six-note figure of the lower line in Example 8c has been changed to a two-note figure (F–G) played in 12/8, and the accents have been placed on every other quarter note. Play the figure in 12/8, as in the first two measures, and accent the cross-rhythm while counting *"one two three, two two three, three two three, four two three."* The next three measures have been rewritten in 2/4 with the quarter note receiving the beat. The phrase is now counted *"one two, one two, one two."* The meter returns to 12/8 in the final measure, counted *"one two three, two two three, three two three, four two three,"* allowing a smooth transition back to the original arpeggio at the top of the example. The two lines together look like this:

```
2/4   1 - and   2 - and   1 - and   2 - and   1 - and   2 - and
12/8  1   2   3,  2   2   3,  3   2   3,  4   2   3
```

Once you get the feel, play the whole example as a loop and try to feel meters and the cross-rythms simultaneously.

Example 9 is an excerpt from an arrangement of the spiritual "Lay This Body Down." The piece is written in 4/4 as a shuffle rhythm, and this passage has a distinct 12/8 feel (though still showing a 4/4 meter) over a 6/4 cross-rhythm. The passage develops by changing the figure and the accents in the bottom line. The lower voice begins with the six-note cross-rhythm figure written as quarter-note triplets in the first two measures. In measures 3 through 5 a third voice emerges that divides the measure in half by accenting a two-note, half-note figure. That third voice ends with a whole note in measure 6. A six-note figure written as quarter-note triplets returns in measure 7. In measure 8 the two-note figure (B–E) is repeated three times. This figure carries over into most of measure 9. Finally, in measures 10 and 11, the cross-rhythm is reversed by having six quarter-note triplets on the top voice played against four quarter notes in the lower voice. This explicitly states the cross-rhythm (six against four), and serves to bring the passage to a cadence—like a closing remark—landing on the sustained chord in the final measure. Set the metronome around 100 bpm and try to feel all the figures while counting in 4/4.

Ex. 8d

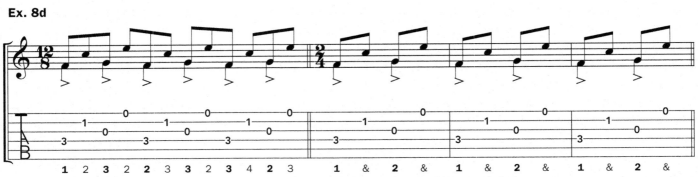

Phrasing

Phrasing is an important aspect of playing any musical instrument. Singers and instrumental soloists find their own way of phrasing a melody, often taking small liberties with timing and pitch to give more character to a line. When playing fingerstyle guitar, phrasing a melody against the accompaniment requires independence between picking-hand fingers—especially between the thumb and fingers—in order to control the volume, articulation, and precise timing of each note. Sometimes the arrangement will specify these details, but very often they are left to the discretion of the player.

Offset Voices

Example 1 is designed to help create awareness of the timing between two voices—one in the bass and one in the melody. Use *p* for the bottom notes, and experiment with different fingers for the top notes. Use the same finger throughout, then alternate fingers. Set the metronome very low (around 52 bpm) and try to hold all notes to their written values.

The offset between the two voices progresses from an eighth note to a 16th note to a 32nd note in the first three measures. In measure 4 the two notes are "flammed"—play them almost, but not quite, at the same time with the bass note on the beat, and the top note as close as possible to the beat, but *just after* it. Play the notes in measure 5 exactly together, then flam the two notes in measure 6 by playing the top note *just before* the bass note is played on the beat. In the last three measures, the offsets progress in reverse order of the first three measures.

As you play Example 1, experiment with the relative volumes of the two notes. Begin by playing the top note louder, and then softer, while keeping the low note at a steady volume. This is generally easier to do when the two notes are separated by time, so practice the difference in volume on the first and last measures, then gradually work toward the middle measures where the two notes are closer together.

In **Example 2**, the melody "Shenandoah" in dropped-D tuning is accompanied by a simple alternating bass of quarter notes that allows you to keep time while focusing on the very simple phrasing of the melody. Play along with a metronome set very slow (♩=80 or less) and play the melody as written, allowing the bass notes to land precisely on the beat. Then try it leaving out all the bass notes on beats two and four. Notice that this makes the melody seem to float a little more freely. (Picking-hand fingerings have been omitted as there are many good options, and it's good practice to develop your own!)

ABOUT TIME
Phrasing

Ex. 2: "Shenandoah"
Dropped-D Tuning: D A D G B E

In **Example 3**, the melody has been rephrased. Articulations have been added and some notes have been offset to sound either earlier or later. The notes that have been offset by an eighth or 16th note sound syncopated, but the ones offset by a 32nd note (marked "flam") have a more flammy sound, and merely approximate a freer phrasing of the melody. The bass keeps a steady quarter-note pattern throughout, except at the end of measure 15 where it anticipates the downbeat of measure 16 by a 32nd note and flams against the next melody note played right on the downbeat.

Experiment with the tempo and with your own changes to the phrasing. Focusing on these small offsets helps train the ear, but in the end, good phrasing often does not require precise mathematical subdivisions, it just requires nudging a note slightly toward or away from the beat. Add some of your own articulations and embellishments. Try leaving out the quarter notes in the bass on beats two and four of some measures and see if that allows you to phrase more freely. Varying the dynamics and the timbre will add even greater expression to your phrasing.

Ex. 3: "Shenandoah"
Dropped-D Tuning: D A D G B E

ABOUT TIME
Phrasing

Stretching/Compressing Time

Sometimes a phrase can be enhanced by intentionally stretching or compressing the durations of a group of notes. The passage from the lullaby "Fais Do-Do" presented earlier takes on a pleasing elastic quality when the notes are not played exactly as written. Example 4 shows a few alternatives for playing the melody on beat three of the opening measure of the piece. **Example 4a** shows the original note values. In **Example 4b**, the hammer-on/pull-off ornament happens in the space of a 16th note instead of the original eighth note. In **Example 4c** the ornament is delayed, and in **Example 4d** the ornament is delayed a 16th note further and written simply as two grace notes with no real time value. Cycle through the variations on the two-measure phrase and experiment with the different note values.

THE ALEX DE GRASSI FINGERSTYLE GUITAR METHOD

Compressing or stretching the tempo of a larger section of music can also be quite effective with some types of music. The original transcription of the "Fais Do-Do" melody is simply marked "freely," but in **Example 5** specific tempo markings have been added to illustrate the point. The first note is marked with a fermata indicating that note should be held, or stretched, longer than its actual written value. Beginning with the third beat of that measure, note values are compressed to bring the phrase first up to tempo (marked *a tempo*), and the compression continues to accelerate (marked *accelerando*) until the *ritard* marking on the second note of the melody in measure 4. There the tempo slows, stretching note values, and hesitates again at the fermata marking at the first melody note in measure 5. The feel is a little like a roller coaster slowly cresting a hill, then accelerating downhill, and then slowing again to a near stop as it crests the next hill. The stretching and compressing should be fluid and feel like a continuous motion. A similar phrasing is marked for the second half of the melody. Play through the whole passage and accelerate and decelerate the tempos as marked, and then experiment with your own phrasing. Try incorporating some of the note value variations from Example 4 on the third beat of measures 1 and 5 as well as the second beat of measures 7 and 9.

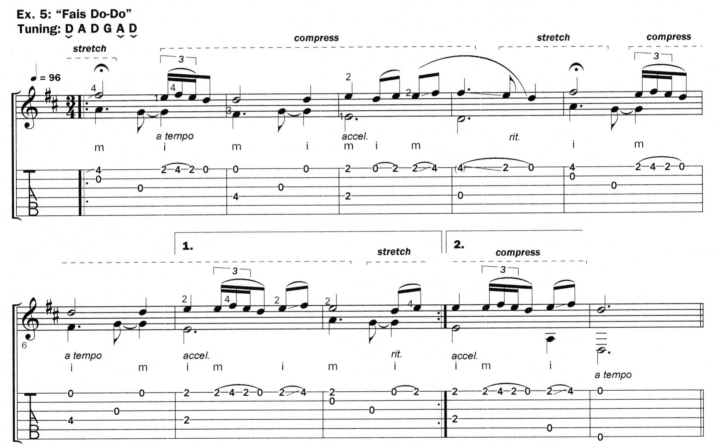

ABOUT TIME
Phrasing

Pulse

Rhythm can be felt as a series of pulses occurring at regular intervals of time. A short pulse marks relatively brief intervals like individual beats, and a long pulse marks longer intervals like two beats, a whole measure, or even multiple measures. However, the notion of short and long is relative. Experiencing the rhythmic pulse at different time intervals allows us to hear a melody as a series of short phrases that link together to make longer phrases.

Example 6 is a "phrasing template" for a 12/8 meter. Tap the notes with your hand, using the accents to group the notes into the short pulse indicated by the brackets above the notes. Tap your foot at the beginning of each bracket below the notes to mark the long pulse. For example, in measure 1, tap the dotted quarter-note beat (every third eighth note) with the foot while tapping and accenting every eighth note with the hand. The hand is marking the very shortest pulse—individual eighth notes. The foot is grouping three eighth notes into a longer dotted-quarter-note pulse. In measure 2, continue to tap every note with the hand, but accent only every third note (dotted quarters). Tap every sixth note (dotted half notes) with the foot. Now the hand is grouping three eighth notes into short dotted-quarter-note pulses, and the foot is grouping two of those three-note pulses into a longer six-note, dotted half pulse. In measure 3, the finger taps every note, accenting every sixth note to create a dotted-half-note pulse, while the foot taps once a measure, grouping 12 notes into a whole-note pulse. The pulses continue to get longer as the exercise progresses, but the pulse tapped out with the hand is always short in relation to the one tapped with the foot. Experiment with combining the various pulses. For example, try tapping the shorter pulses of measures 1 and 2 with the longer pulses in later measures and vice-versa.

Next, try singing the triplets "da-da-da" throughout the exercise, observing the accents that coincide with the shorter pulse. In measure 1, every note is accented; in measure 2 only every beat is accented; and so on. The phrasing starts out very choppy but becomes more fluid as the pulses become longer.

Ex. 6

(cont'd)

THE ALEX DE GRASSI FINGERSTYLE GUITAR METHOD **163**

Example 6 functions as a template for experimenting with the phrasing in the excerpt from my composition "Children's Dance" in **Example 7**. The passage is very symmetrical. It consists of four two-measure phrases in a typical ABAC form, with the first and third phrase being the same and the fourth phrase being a variation of the second phrase. But, the phrasing can be further shaped by feeling the pulses that coincide with the space between strong downbeats and the accented notes. For example, in measures 1–2 and 5–6 the first pulse spans two beats, the second spans four beats, and the third and fourth span a single beat each. Try tapping your foot at the beginning of each of those pulses, and notice how it creates a rhythmic pattern for the phrase of:

The second phrase comprises a two-beat pulse and a six-beat pulse, or dotted-half, dotted-half tied to dotted-whole pattern. The fourth phrase in measures 7–8 can be felt as a dotted-half, dotted-half, dotted-quarter, dotted-quarter, dotted-quarter, dotted-quarter series of pulses.

Tap your foot on the pulses as marked by the dashed lines to help you feel the phrasing as you play through the passage. Then play the passage feeling the pulse at symmetrical intervals like every one, two, four, or eight beats. Observe how the notes seem choppy and disconnected with the shortest pulse and how they become more connected into a long fluid phrases as the pulses get longer. Experiment with your own phrasing.

Feeling the short pulse is often helpful for executing individual notes accurately and with a precise timing. Feeling longer pulses helps connect the music into more fluid phrases and melodies in a way that provides continuity for a seamless performance. These are both important elements. Successful phrasing often sounds free and takes liberties with compressing or stretching time, but it is also dependent on feeling the rhythmic pulse at different intervals.

Section 10
Extended Techniques

Percussion 166

Slapping and Tapping 172

Audio Playlist 2, Tracks 67–89

Methods of producing sounds on the guitar that require something more than plucking and fretting notes are often called *extended techniques*. The term is always being redefined as innovation makes yesterday's extended techniques tomorrow's fundamentals. Extended techniques fall into two major categories that might be classified as 1) percussion techniques played on the body and strings of the guitar, and 2) two hands on the fingerboard techniques, or tapping/slapping. Because many of these techniques are new and evolving, the notation is not entirely standardized.

Percussion

The body of the guitar makes a pretty good percussion instrument. It's a hollow box, not unlike a drum, and it can produce a variety of sounds depending on where and how it's struck. Most guitars are remarkably sturdy as well, though there are no guarantees.

Tambor

The terms *tambor* (meaning "drum" in Spanish, *tambora* in Italian) and *golpe* (strike) have been used for some time as directions in classical guitar repertoire—most notably South American music (such as tango and other dance rhythms). Typically, the player is meant to strike the picking-hand thumb at one of three locations: directly on the bridge, somewhere on the soundboard, or on the strings just in front of the saddle. *Tambor* is typically indicated by an *X* with a stem in the notation (usually on the first space) and by an *X* in the tablature. The words *tambor* or *golpe* are written above the staff.

To play *tambor*, the picking-hand arm needs to shift somewhat so it rests on the upper bout closer to the back of guitar. The picking hand should be open, hovering about an inch (2–3 cm) above the top, with the thumb extended straight. In preparation, rotate the wrist so the thumb lifts away from the guitar, then rotate the hand back toward the guitar and strike the thumb against the bridge (see photo). Then, with the hand even closer to the back of the guitar, practice striking the top at locations behind the bridge and listen to the variations in tone. A somewhat lower, thuddier sound is produced when the heel of the hand rests on the top.

Example 1 shows a typical tango rhythm (approximately 120–132 bpm). Muting the strings by immobilizing them with the fretting hand yields the purest drum sound. However, sometimes it's desirable to let the strings ring. **Example 2** integrates strummed chords with drumming. Let the first two chords ring and continue drumming till the next chord. Stop the strings abruptly with the fretting hand after the third chord and continue

TRACK 67

Ex. 1

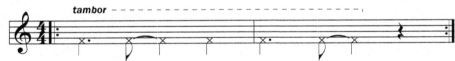

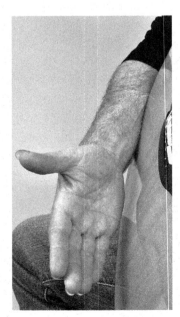 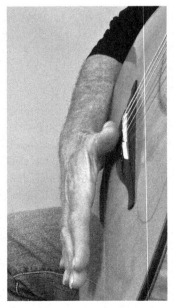

To play *tambor*, keep the thumb straight and strike it against the bridge.

EXTENDED TECHNIQUES
Percussion

drumming till the repeat. Experiment with striking both the bridge and the guitar top.

The *tambor* or *golpe* can also indicate striking the strings directly with the picking-hand thumb just in front of the saddle. With the fretting hand immobilizing the strings and the picking-hand thumb continuing to rest across all the strings after the *golpe* (see photo), you can achieve a muted drum sound with very little string resonance. Quickly withdrawing *p* after striking the strings produces a more resonant drum sound. If the fretting hand is either off the strings or holding a chord, the open strings, or the chord, will sound in addition to a more lively drum sound (see photo). Play the first two measures of **Example 3** with strings muted, and in measures 3 and 4 allow the chords to ring.

Ex. 2

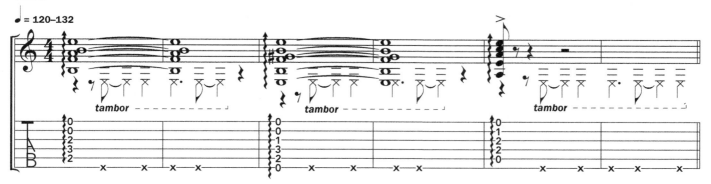

Ex. 3

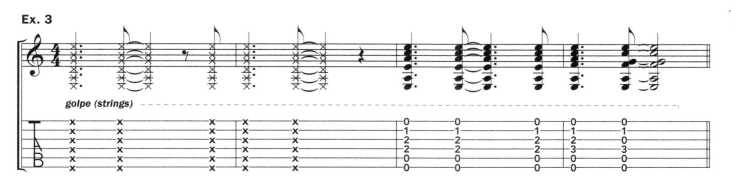

Playing *golpe* with the fretting hand stopping the strings results in a muted drum sound.

A more lively drum sound results from playing *golpe* with the strings open.

The strings will be more resonant as the picking moves closer to the soundhole.

The Drum Kit

Drumming on the guitar body can approximate the sound of a drum kit—kick (bass) drum, snare, toms, and hi-hat—by striking different areas of the guitar and strings. There is no "standardized" guitar-percussion notation as yet, but one solution is to use a type of percussion notation that assigns each sound to a specific space on the five-line staff, as shown in **Example 4a**. Though these sounds do not have a defined pitch, they are arranged bottom to top in order from low to high sounds.

To avoid confusion and clutter with notes on the standard guitar staff, the guitar percussion can be written on an additional staff. This can either be a five-line staff, a three-line staff, or, as shown in **Example 4b**, a single-line staff as is sometimes used in percussion notation.

The kick-drum sound can be played with the thumb striking the top of the guitar a few inches behind the bridge, usually closer to the lower bout. The higher-pitched tom sound can be found on the top closer to the edge. The still-higher-pitched snare sound can be produced by striking the side of the guitar.

To have access to all three sounds from one hand position (more or less), place the palm of the picking hand near the edge of the guitar about halfway between the butt of the guitar and the lower bout. The thumb rests on the top and the fingers fold over the edge of the guitar at the knuckles, resting on the side (see photo). To play the kick sound, raise *p* by rotating the hand slightly, then bring it down rapidly to strike the top. With the hand in the starting position, and without moving the hand, raise (straighten out) the *a* finger (the other fingers will likely move some as well) and slap the side of the guitar. Keep the finger straight and accelerate it quickly—the bone mass should make a bright, resonant woody sound.

Ex. 4a

Ex. 4b

Place the picking hand on the edge of the guitar, halfway between the butt of the guitar and the lower bout, to play kick drum, tom, and snare sounds.

Play the basic rock pattern in **Example 5** while concentrating on getting a good kick and snare sound. The thumb should be kept straight and extended at least a couple inches in toward the center of the top. It may be necessary to move your hand somewhat in order to reach a good, low sound on the kick. Try it both with the fretting hand muting the strings and with the strings open.

With the hand in the same position, strike the thumb on the top near the edge (within an inch, or, 2–3 cm) to get the tom sound. The pitch should be somewhere between the kick and snare pitches. A lighter tom sound can also be played with one or more fingers by moving the whole hand onto the top. The pitch will vary depending on which finger is used and the precise location it strikes. Experiment with different locations and find some sounds that work for you. **Example 6** uses the *i* and *m* fingers to incorporate a tom sound into the basic rock pattern.

Triplets/Rolls/Flams

The tom sound is useful for playing triplets, flams, and rolls with the fingers. With the picking hand in the same position used for Example 6 (on top of the guitar), try playing a series of eighth-note triplets in a 4/4 shuffle rhythm using the *a* finger to strike the edge of the guitar top as shown in measure 1 of **Example 7**. Give the first note of each triplet a slight accent. Try using the *m* and *i* fingers as well. In measure 2, the second and triple are divided into two 16th notes using *i* and *m* (counting one, two-*and*, three). In measure 3 the second triplet of beats one and three is divided into three 16th-note triplets using *a, m,* and *i*. The first of the 16th-note triplets gets the accent and other two are "rolled" as if the three notes were one continuous action.

When moving between the tom and snare sounds, it's often more convenient to play the tom with the thumb, as shown in measure 1 of the shuffle rhythm (swing notation) in **Example 8**. The hand doesn't need to move much for the thumb to cover both kick and tom sounds. In second half of measure 2, the snare is not played and the tom fill is played with the fingers. Note that the eighth notes are swung, so the offbeats are felt more like the third beat of a triplet.

Example 9 (page 170) uses a very similar shuffle-rhythm pattern as a percussion fill to segue between verses of my D A D G A D arrangement of the spiritual "Lay This Body Down." The percussion is on its own stave. In measure 2, the eighth-note triplet on beat three contains a nested 16th-note triplet on the second eighth note, followed by a rest on the third eighth-note triplet. Practice that measure very slowly, counting out each eighth-note triplet. By slightly changing the position of the fingers between the nested triplet and the final eighth-note triplet on beat four of the measure, you can approximate a sense of

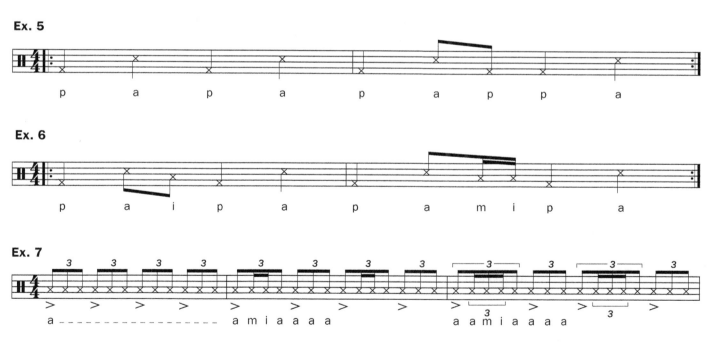

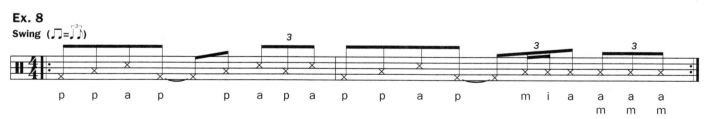

Ex. 9: "Lay This Body Down"
Tuning: D A D G A D

moving between two differently pitched tom drums. (Remember, the *X* note head on beat four of measure 5 and beat two of measure 6 in the top stave, the notation, is just a slapped bass note as described in Example 6 of "More Patterns.")

Strumming can be combined with percussion to create a strong rhythm groove. **Example 10** uses a hip-hop rhythm with a simple chord progression. The chords are strummed mostly with the flesh of the thumb, allowing the hand to stay open as it moves quickly between drumming and strumming. The percussion (tom sound) notes played with *m* coming one eighth note before the strums should be executed with an upward sweep of the picking hand, moving it into position for the strum that follows.

There are other ways of playing percussion sounds that keep the hand closer to the strings. Closing the picking hand into a fist and striking the heel of the hand against the top just above the soundhole on the bridge side, produces a low thud (kick sound). This is graphically represented by a solid square, the same symbol sometimes used for *tambor*. If the backs of the fingers (of the closed fist) are allowed to simultaneously strike the strings, a sound similar to a hi-hat or a snare drum is also produced. That sound is graphically represented by a rectangle with a diagonal line through it placed just above the kick drum symbol. The hi-hat sound can also be played independently of the kick drum sound. For more clarity, the fretting hand can be used to mute the

EXTENDED TECHNIQUES
Percussion

strings. **Example 11** demonstrates the two used together in a simple rhythmic pattern.

The flick is a somewhat modified flamenco technique that works well for striking one or more strings with a very sharp attack. It is graphically represented by the symbol shown in **Example 12**, with the picking-hand finger to be used (typically *m*) below. To execute the flick, curl the finger into the palm of the hand. Use the flesh of the palm to load a little tension on the finger, then flick the finger down to strike the string or chord indicated. This technique can be successfully combined with the soundhole-position kick drum and hi-hat sounds all at once as shown in Example 12. Practice the flick in measure 1, and then together with the kick drum and hi-hat as indicated in measure 2.

A variety of percussion sounds are combined with strums and flicks into a rock-blues riff in **Example 13**.

Slapping and Tapping

String-slapping techniques can be used for both percussive effect and to produce individual notes and chords. Slaps can be executed with an outstretched picking-hand finger at any location on the strings. When the slap is over the fingerboard, specific frets may be indicated. The slap is graphically represented by the word *slap* below or above the notes to be slapped. The note(s) may be accompanied by a picking-hand fingering—if not, *i* is the default finger.

With the extended picking hand resting either on the top of the guitar or about an inch above the top, raise the hand by bending the wrist back and then slap the hand across the strings near the bridge with the *i* finger. Moving your picking hand slowly toward the fingerboard as you continue slapping will cause the timbre to change as different overtones are emphasized. If the palm of the hand is allowed to come down and strike the top of the guitar as the finger slaps the strings, an additional low-drum (kick) sound is produced. Slapping over the fingerboard adds the percussive sounds of the strings pressing against the frets, and also the sound of the slapping finger bouncing off of the fingerboard (see photo). These percussive effects may be indicated by the kick drum or hi-hat symbols but often are not. Experiment by slapping the open strings at different locations—from near the bridge to over the frets—as shown in **Example 1**.

String slapping can be used simply for percussion, but it is more commonly used to play notes and harmonics. The chords in **Example 2** are held with the fretting hand while the *i* finger slaps only the indicated strings. This requires adjusting the angle of the index finger relative to the plane of the strings (see photo). For the individual notes in measure 4, the *i* finger needs to bend in order for the fingertip joint to come down more perpendicular to the strings. The very end of the fingertip slaps the string. It takes some practice to develop the precision to avoid slapping strings not to be played. Available fretting-hand fingers can also be used to mute open strings.

Ex. 1
Tuning: D A D G A D

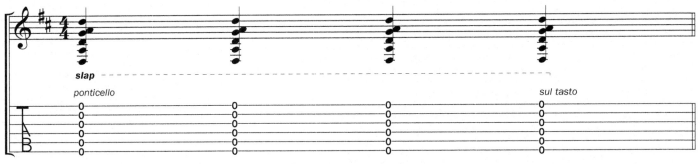

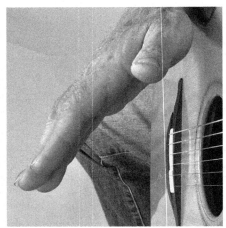

Slaps can be executed by bending the wrist back and slapping the strings with your index finger.

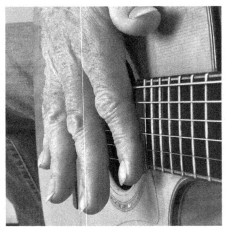

Adjust the angle of the index finger to slap the strings indicated in Example 2.

EXTENDED TECHNIQUES
Slapping and Tapping

Ex. 2
Tuning: D A D G A D

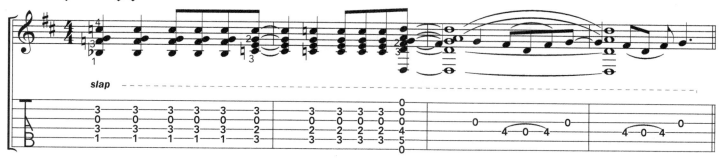

Slapped Harmonics

Both natural and artificial harmonics can be produced with the slapping technique. The standard harmonic symbols—the diamond note head in the notation, and the dot in the tab—are accompanied by the word *slap, S.H.,* or sometimes *T* (for tap) or other explanatory text. For chords or single notes composed only of natural harmonics, the frets to be slapped are simply shown in the tab with a dot, brackets, or some type of enclosure indicating harmonics. For artificial harmonics, or chords containing both harmonics and regular notes, the tab displays the position of the fretting hand directly below the notation, and the frets to be slapped (all notes are slapped) to trigger harmonics are shown in brackets just to the right. (Sometimes 0's will be displayed for natural harmonics to indicate the strings are open, but they are not necessary.) Typically the picking-hand finger will bounce off the fingerboard, creating an additional percussive sound. The palm may also strike the top, adding the low kick-drum sound, and this may be additionally notated with a solid square.

Example 3 shows a series of slapped harmonic chords at various positions on the fingerboard. The first occurs at a natural harmonic node (12th fret), and the second and third are slapped artificial harmonics played 12 frets up from a barre played with the fretting hand at the third and fifth frets, respectively. The fourth chord (anticipating the third measure) combines artificial harmonics (12 frets up from notes fretted at the third fret) with nonharmonic pitches (the open strings and notes fretted at the first fret). The final chord leaves the fretting hand in the same position, but becomes a new chord when slapped at the 12th fret. Combining harmonics with normal notes is a very effective method for creating unusual chord voicings with a big range. For example, with conventional techniques it would be difficult to play the E♭ and B♭ in the bass in D A D G A D and reach the high C and D notes as shown in measures 2, 3, and 4.

Slapping techniques can be combined with more conventional techniques like hammer-ons and pull-offs to good effect. **Example 4** (page 174), a passage from "Blue Trout," utilizes all of the slapping techniques above. Beginning at letter C at measure 5, all the stems-up notes and chords are slapping with the index finger. The bass notes (except for the "hammer-on from nowhere" chord on the downbeat of measure 17—to be discussed in the tapping section ahead) are all slapped with the thumb using the slapped percussion technique presented in "More Patterns." Note the interplay of slapped harmonics and slapped nonharmonics with hammer-ons and pull-offs.

Ex. 3
Tuning: D A D G A D

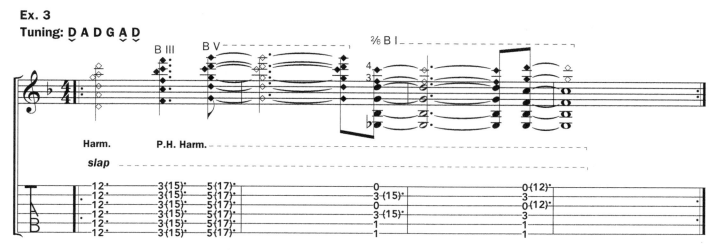

Ex. 4: "Blue Trout"
Tuning: D A D G A D

174 THE ALEX DE GRASSI FINGERSTYLE GUITAR METHOD

EXTENDED TECHNIQUES
Slapping and Tapping

Tapping

Tapped notes are initiated with a single hand using a "hammer-on from nowhere" technique, thus eliminating the need to pluck the string with the other hand. The hammer-on from nowhere can be executed with either hand, or both hands together. Tapping evolved as an electric-guitar technique, and a major challenge for tapping on an acoustic guitar is to produce sufficient volume and quality of tone that integrates seamlessly with conventionally plucked notes and other techniques.

Hammer-ons from nowhere are graphically represented by a short tie-like symbol connected to the left side of notes and tab numbers, and either a fretting-hand (1–4) or picking-hand fingering (*p, i, m, a, c*) to designate the hand and finger used.

The hammer-on from nowhere is executed as a somewhat exaggerated hammer-on. The fretting-hand finger may need to be lifted above the fingerboard higher than for normal hammer-ons in order to attack the string with greater force and speed, thus setting the string in motion and producing a clear pitch. The note is then sustained for the written duration, and can be given articulations like vibrato, etc. Like any other note, tapped notes are "live" and can be followed by a pull-off, a normal hammer-on, or any other way of playing a note. Pay close attention to the distinction between hammer-ons from nowhere and the other hammer-ons, pull-offs, and slides in **Example 5**. Note that the last note of the example (the higher D in measure 4) is plucked with the index finger. All other notes are played with the fretting-hand fingers indicated.

Tip for Example 5: To control unwanted resonance and achieve greater clarity, begin with the picking-hand fingers resting on strings 1–3 and *p* covering the bottom three strings. Lift *i* off the string as the fretting-hand index finger hammers down. Replace *i* for the eighth-note rest and repeat through measure 1.

In measure 2 of the example, uncover the fourth string and stop the third string with *i* as the fourth string is tapped. In measure 3, leave *p* on string 6 and mute string 4 with finger 3 as it plays the fifth string (see fretting-hand muting in the Section 3 lesson "Note Duration"). Move *p* to strings 4 and 5 to play the first three notes of measure 4, then pluck the fourth string with *i* at the same time that the fretting hand pulls off—both notes sound simultaneously. Damping any unwanted resonance will allow the tapped notes to "speak" more clearly.

To tap notes with the picking hand, place the picking-hand thumb on the upper edge of the fingerboard at an angle of approximately 30 degrees. This supports the tapping fingers. The thumb should be relaxed, relatively straight, and not touching the sixth string. It should be stationary but also able to move easily between positions, generally keeping one or two frets closer to the bridge than the notes being tapped. The tapping finger is "cocked" by opening the hand, recoiling the finger, then attacking the string with force and speed. The last two joints straighten out as the finger comes down right behind the fret (see photo). The fingertip impacts the string at approximately a 60-degree angle, allowing the picking-hand fingernail (which should not be too long!) to stay clear of the string and fingerboard. This impact angle will vary depending on what's being played, size of the hand, etc. Picking-hand tapped notes are designated with *p, i, m, a,* and *c* fingerings—placed near the note head or tab number for clarity—along with the tie-like symbol indicating that they are tapped notes. Picking-hand tapped notes are often used together with fretting-hand tapped notes.

Cock the tapping finger and then attack the string with the picking-hand fingertip at about a 60 degree angle to the fingerboard.

Ex. 5
Tuning: D A D G A D

Example 6 begins with the picking hand positioned somewhere between the eighth and the ninth fret in preparation for tapping at the seventh fret. The fretting hand is held in second position, covering the first five strings to control resonance until needed for the hammer-on. The picking hand taps the note, holds it for an eighth note, then pulls off to the open string. The fretting hand then covers all six strings during the rests. The fretting-hand fingers hammer the third and fourth notes (F and G) in measure 2. The A♭ on beat three is tapped with *i*, but note that it is slurred, thus a normal hammer-on—not a hammer-on from nowhere. Measures 3 and 4 progress to the fifth and fourth strings with an interplay of fretting hand and picking hand in a series of tapped notes. The *i* below the low D indicates that *i* should pluck the open sixth string from the picking-hand tapping position. This happens at the same time that the fretting hand slides to the D an octave above. Practice the exercise with the repeat as a continual loop, striving for evenness of volume and tone.

More than one musical line may be tapped simultaneously. Paying close attention to note durations, phrasing, and articulations will give each line more independence. The hands may cross over so that each hand taps notes in both lines, as shown in **Example 7**.

Tapped Chords

Whole chords can be played with a single hand or a combination of hands. In **Example 8**, the octaves in the bass line are tapped using a combination of fretting-hand fingers 2 and 3, and picking-hand fingers *i* and *m*. Then, while the picking hand holds the bass notes, the fretting-hand *i* finger hammers down a partial barre on the top four strings to complete the Gm7 chord in measure 1. Note that in order for the F on the fourth string to sound, *m* must let go of that string just prior to the hammered barre with the fretting hand. In measure 3 the picking hand executes a partial barre across strings 5 and 6. To execute this move, *p* continues to rest on the edge of the fingerboard, but the wrist, forearm,

176 THE ALEX DE GRASSI FINGERSTYLE GUITAR METHOD

EXTENDED TECHNIQUES
Slapping and Tapping

and hand rotate toward the player to allow *i* to become parallel to the fingerboard. With the picking-hand fingers together for support, the side (toward the thumb) of *i* hammers down to fret strings 5 and 6. While the picking hand holds that position, the fretting-hand fingers 2, 3, and 4 form a shape above the fingerboard and hammer down to complete the Aadd11 chord.

Getting chords to sound with clarity and volume is a challenge. As with individual notes, some of the energy in producing notes is lost to the vibration toward the nut side of the fretted position—the so-called back vibration. This becomes more problematic higher up the fingerboard. Tapping onto a previously fretted note or position does seem to eliminate some of the back vibration and improves the purity of tone. This works well when a note is tapped as a hammer-on from a previous note. However, the other hand is not always available for that purpose, unless the arranger has factored that into the arrangement. (Some players have attempted to modify the nut or mute the strings where they pass over the nut to minimize back vibration.)

Just as the picking hand can fret notes on the fingerboard, the fretting hand can reverse roles and be used to mimic picking-hand techniques such as strumming and slapping. The same graphic symbols are used as for the picking hand. They are distinguished only by fingerings. In **Example 9** the first barre chord is a hammer-on from nowhere played with the first fretting-hand finger. The second chord is sounded by an down-strum executed by dragging the same finger across all six strings slowly enough to sound the open string notes in rapid succession (indicated by the 1 and the squiggly arrow—see photo). The fretting-hand thumb remains stationary for support as the rest of the hand pulls away from the guitar and the finger gradually recoils.

In measure 2, the first fretting-hand finger hammers down a barre across strings 1–4, allowing open strings 5 and 6 to continue to ring. Then the same finger pulls away in one quick motion (as indicated by the straight arrow with the 1 next to it), while the *i* finger lightly barres at the seventh fret in order to trigger the natural harmonics at that node. In measures 3 and 4 the harmonics are slapped with the third fretting-hand finger—a bracket indicates it slaps across all six strings.

Tapping, slapping, percussion, and plucked notes are all integrated with an up-tempo swing rhythm in the excerpt from my composition "The Monkulator" in **Example 10** on the next page. The transcription has become sufficiently complex to merit the use of separate staves for the notation. (Some transcriptions in the tapping style use two staves of tablature as well, but here only one is used.) Keep in mind the two notation staves are not necessarily unique to picking hand and fretting hand—both hands play notes in both staves.

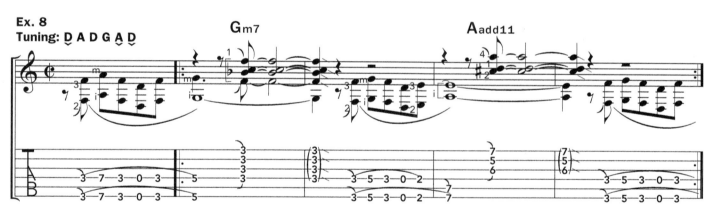

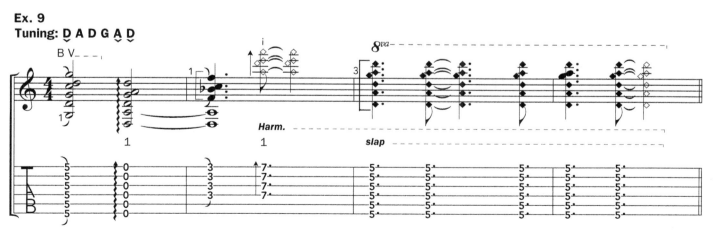

The tuning, D A D F G C, allows for some interesting jazz chord voicings. Note that the slapped chords in measure 3 combine both natural and artificial harmonics with the nonharmonic pitch (G♯ at the third fret). The slapped chords in measures 7 and 11 combine natural harmonics with nonharmonic pitches. The percussion breaks in measures 4 and 8 are played with the picking-hand thumb on the top of the guitar, just above the soundhole. Playing near the curve of the upper bout yields a brighter sound, and playing closer to the soundhole gives more of the kick-drum sound.

Ex. 10: "The Monkulator"
Tuning: D A D F G C

* Picking-hand thumb strikes the top of the guitar, just above the soundhole.

178 THE ALEX DE GRASSI FINGERSTYLE GUITAR METHOD

Section 11
The 3-D Sound

Depth of Field 180

Orchestration 184

Audio Playlist 2, Tracks 90–99

Though we can't see it, sound occurs in a three-dimensional realm. We can spatially locate and differentiate most sounds in the dark or with our eyes closed. Likewise, when listening to a band or orchestra, we can place the sounds of various instruments in a three-dimensional sound field based on sound quality, volume, and physical location. Because the guitar is a polyphonic instrument with the capacity for a wide range of sonorities and textures, it's possible to place different notes in a sound field and orchestrate them in a similar way. It can even be quite helpful to imagine the different voices in a guitar arrangement being played on different instruments, each with its unique timbre, articulations, and dynamics.

In this section, we'll look at ways of adding depth and dimension to your playing using the concepts of "depth of field" and orchestration. Along the way we'll be revisiting some of the techniques and idioms presented in previous lessons and attempting to put them together in the larger context of orchestrating the 3-D sound.

Depth of Field

The concept of *depth of field* is used by photographers to arrange objects spatially in a photograph. The subject in the foreground is given a sense of depth by including the wall in the middle ground and the horizon in the distant background. The viewer's immediate attention is fixed on the subject, but gradually moves to the wall and still later the horizon. Similarly, in music different voices can be positioned at different depths in an imaginary sound field—for example the melody in the foreground, the bass in the middle ground, and the accompaniment or the echo of a countermelody in the background. In fact, each note could be considered to be like a pixel in the photograph with its own weight or density, and its own coordinates in a 3-D sound field. Recording engineers often speak of positioning sounds within a stereo image or even a surround sound field.

Depth of field is accomplished primarily through "internal dynamics"—the relative volume or weight given to each voice or even to each individual note. Finding that balance in a guitar arrangement is a powerful tool for creating a moving performance. It's challenging to play juxtaposed voices, or even simultaneous notes, at different volumes. The key to controlling these internal dynamics is learning to deliver the right touch, with its own individual volume, to every note. I call this the *hierarchy of accents*.

The first group of examples is intended to help develop awareness and train the fingers to vary the volume in a hierarchy of accents. **Example 1a** is a tremolo pattern—four groups of 16th notes repeating the same note—with an accent on each beat. The picking-hand fingering, a three-stroke *a–m–i* sequence, requires the accent to be played by a different finger each time. Play the example slowly with a metronome and exaggerate the accents while playing the other notes softly. Once you can play it smoothly, try it at faster tempos. Then try measure 2—without any accents. Strive to play the tremolo fluidly with every note at the same volume. (It's worth noting that the lesser tension of nylon strings makes it easier to play tremolo. The technique is used to good effect on classical guitar to sustain long notes—usually in con-

Absolute and Apparent Note Durations

Note durations can be controlled *absolutely* by string-stopping techniques, or notes can have an *apparent* duration defined by their volume relative to the other notes—even though they may continue to sound beyond their written value. These two means of controlling durations can be used in combination. This is particularly noticeable when melody and bass lines are integrated with arpeggios. Melody and bass are given an absolute duration because the strings can be stopped, released, or reactivated readily. The durations of the remaining notes of the arpeggio accompaniment are more difficult to control, but, because they are played softly, they may *appear* to have only eighth note values.

Ex. 1a

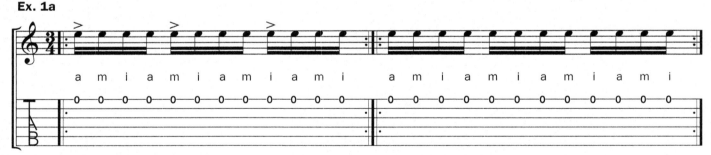

Ex. 1b

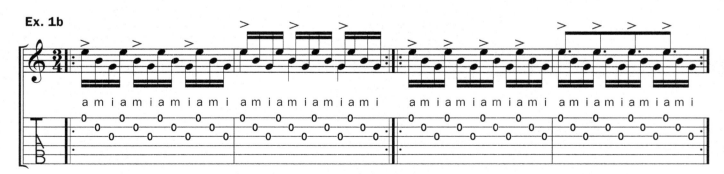

THE 3-SOUND
Depth of Field

trast to a second voice played with *p*. Playing tremolo smoothly and musically on steel-string guitars takes considerably more effort.)

The offset between the fingering pattern and note groupings becomes more apparent in **Example 1b**. A four-note arpeggio is repeated using *a–m–i*, but the accent is placed on every fourth note—on the beat. Accent the downbeat of each arpeggio heavily, and play the other notes softly. Let all the notes ring, and notice how the accents outline a simple, on-the-beat quarter note figure E–B–G, with each quarter note plucked with a different finger. This has been rewritten in measure 2 to show the figure as a separate voice. In measure 3 the accents have been placed on every *a* stroke, resulting in a syncopated, dotted-eighth note figure that creates a four-against-three cross-rhythm figure (see the About Time section for review) consisting of repeated E notes. Measure 4 has been rewritten to show the cross-rhythm as a separate voice. Keep counting in 3/4.

In **Example 2a** the fretting-hand fingering sequence *i–m–a* is used throughout. The accents are on the first 16th of each beat, creating a quarter note melody. The fingers used to play the melody rotate from *i* to *m* to *a* throughout. In fact, these accented notes need to be released before their full quarter note value so other notes can be played; but, when accented heavily, they have an *apparent* value of quarter notes. The same sequence of notes is shown in **Example 2b** with the accents placed on every third 16th note, creating a syncopated, dotted-eighth note melody and

THE ALEX DE GRASSI FINGERSTYLE GUITAR METHOD

a four-against-three cross-rhythm. Every melody note begins with *i*. Be sure to play all the accented notes loud with *absolute* durations and the other notes softly with *apparent* durations. Let all the notes ring.

Try tapping your foot on the beat of the accented notes of Example 2b. The beat now falls every third 16th note and the passage could be rewritten in 12/8, as shown in **Example 3**. It's the same sequence of notes played with the same fingering and accents—just a different way of hearing the rhythm.

The previous arpeggios in this lesson are played with *i, m,* and *a* and suggest two voices, one accented and the other played softly. The arpeggio excerpted from my arrangement of the spiritual "Lay This Body Down" in **Example 4** adds the thumb into the mix and suggests three or even four voices, depending on how the player interprets it. The piece is written in common 4/4, but this passage, with eighth note triplets throughout, suggests 12/8. The thumb plays the quarter note triplet cross-rhythm.

Ex. 3

Ex. 4: "Lay This Body Down"
Tuning: D A D G A D

THE 3-D SOUND
Depth of Field

Hearing Voices

This orchestration example illustrates how to hear and identify the various parts of the arrangement. The first line shows the guitar notation of the passage, with the tab below. The four staves below show the individual voices that have been extracted from the transcription (without the addition of any notes). Voice 1 consists of the high accented notes. Voice 2 is the cross-rhythm counter-figure. Voice 3 consists of the long, sustained bass notes tied over the bar line. The arpeggio, complete with notes not included in voices 1–3, could be considered a separate voice 4.

Imagine the four separate voices assigned to four different instruments in a quartet. Let's say voice 1 is violin, voice 2 is cello, voice 3 is bass, and voice 4 is piano (optional).

In that scenario, the bass would most likely play down an octave, the violin up an octave, and the piano perhaps up an octave. The quartet would thus be able to extend the range of pitch and undoubtedly each instrument would add expression unique to that particular instrument as well.

Note that the violin part (more rhythm than melody) is marked *double forte*, the cello part is marked *mezzo-piano,* and the bass is marked *mezzo-forte,* with hairpins indicating a gradually decay of each note. The optional piano part is marked *piano*.

Try to apply these dynamics to each voice as you play the guitar passage to establish a hierarchy of accents: voice 1 loud, voice 2 soft, and voice 3 somewhere in between 1 and 2. Once you've got that, play with the balance and vary the internal dynamics.

Notice that some of the notes function in more than one voice. The cello part includes the notes that the bass plays but doesn't sustain the low notes. It repeats the first note of each measure while the bass part is tied over. You can suggest tied notes by playing the bass notes in measures 1 and 3 louder than the repetition of those notes by the cello on beat one of measures 2 and 4. The piano plays all the notes, including some not played by the other voices, without accenting or sustaining any of the notes. This is a somewhat conceptual, abstract voice. It's impossible to play all the other parts and play voice 4 with all unaccented eighth notes—it's merely a way to hear the whole arpeggio as a part or voice of its own.

This orchestration also shows the various rhythmic elements at work. For example, voice 2 plays the countermelody that suggests 6/4 (six quarter-note triplets per measure), voice 3 carries the 4/4, and the piano spells out the 12/8 feel. Voice 1 adds a syncopated motif.

Orchestration

In the last lesson we imagined the voices in a piece of music as different instruments in a quartet—violin, cello, bass, and piano—with different dynamic markings. Now imagine how that quartet might actually sound when each instrument has its own articulations and expressions.

The violin is the brightest instrument, and it's directed to play with a brittle *ponticello* attack. The cello has a warmer tone but is directed to play *marcato* (marked, emphatic). The bass has the darkest sound and is played *arco*, bowing long notes. To suggest these different timbres and articulations on the guitar, play voice 1 notes *ponticello*, voice 2 notes closer to the soundhole but with some nail for definition, and the voice 3 notes *sul tasto*, maybe with the flesh of the thumb. To get more spatial separation between picking-hand thumb and fingers, lower the angle of the picking-hand thumb to extend it farther toward the soundhole for voice 3 notes (see "The Picking Hand").

Example 4 in the "Depth of Field" lesson deconstructed a existing musical phrase. Now we'll build one from the ground up. **Example 1a** is a simple repeated arpeggio. As a warm-up to bring some awareness to the picking-hand fingers, play the example and shift the accent back one eighth note with each repetition as indicated. In **Example 1b**, some additional accented notes are added. Play the arpeggio softly and emphasize the accented notes to put them in the foreground, letting all the strings ring freely.

In **Example 1c** the phrase has been rewritten to define note durations and assign notes to separate voices. Voice 1 is the melody, voice 2 is the bass line, and voice 3 includes the remaining notes of the original arpeggio. Establish a hierarchy of accents by playing voice 1 the loudest, voice 2 at moderate volume, and the remaining notes of the arpeggio, voice 3, very softly. Then, focus on both picking-hand and fretting-hand string-stopping techniques to control the note durations of the melody and the bass—fretted notes can be held and released, and open strings can be stopped with the finger that plucked them. The remaining notes of the arpeggio, voice 3, can be stopped, but it may sound more fluid to simply play them very softly and allow them to ring with apparent eighth-note durations. Resetting the picking hand at the beginning of each measure will also help control resonance and add clarity.

The next step is to apply the articulations to the melody as indicated in **Example 1d**. The sequence of staccato, no articulation, then vibrato gives some shape to the melody in the first measure. The long vibrato note F♯ in measure 1 is answered by the texture of the long open-string note E in measure 2. Measure 3 has the same articulation as measure 1, then the last three notes of measure 4 are played staccato by quickly releasing the fretted notes. This staccato effect will speak through more clearly when the bass note is held to its absolute dotted quarter note value.

In **Example 1e**, dynamics and timbre expressions have been added. Starting at *mezzo-piano* the phrase gradually crescendos to *forte* by the beginning of measure 3, then it decrescendos to *piano* by the end of measure 4. At the same time, the picking

Ex. 1a

THE 3-D SOUND
Orchestration

hand is gradually moving from *sul tasto* near the soundhole to *metalico* near the bridge. Remember, while the volume is increasing and decreasing over the four measures, the internal dynamics—the relative volume between the three voices—should stay the same. This takes serious concentration but is very good practice for keeping the depth of field and 3-D sound consistent!

Once you have the dynamics and timbre expressions down, check to see that you're also applying note durations and articulations properly. There's a lot to think about in this example. Once you've mastered Example 1e, reviewing the whole example will give some perspective on how this process can be applied to almost any fingerstyle arrangement.

Examples 2–5 consist of short excerpts from the transcription of my composition "Western" in D A D G C E♭ tuning. The individual voices have been extracted and placed on separate staves below the transcription to help illustrate the concept of orchestration. The key signature is E♭, making good use of the open first string in contrast to fretted notes.

In **Example 2**, the *m* and *a* fingers play two notes together—unisons on beat two, and a somewhat dissonant minor second on the third beat. The *fretted* E♭ and D notes comprise the "true" melody (voice 1). Those *m* finger notes can be emphasized over the drone-like *a* finger notes played on the open-string E♭ (voice 2). By using a bit more force with the *m* finger (*fortissimo*), observing the grace note, and adding a small amount of pitch modulation, voice 1 can be phrased independently of the voice 2 drone harmony. The second note of voice 1 in measures 2 and 4 is played staccato, in contrast to the voice 2 drone notes marked *tenuto*, indicating they should be held for their whole value. The bass notes (voice 3) are played with flesh of the thumb somewhat softer (*mezzo-forte*), and the repeating B♭ (voice 4) in the middle is played very softly (*mezzo-piano*) with the *i* finger. (Using picking-hand string stopping to hold voice 4 notes to their written duration will further distinguish them.) This hierarchy of accents and the contrasting articulations balance the voices, working together to orchestrate and phrase the music successfully. Note that voices 1 and 3 converge momentarily when they share the eighth-note B♭ at the end of measures 2 and 4.

A little later in the piece the harmonized melody becomes syncopated—sounding on the offbeats. In **Example 3** the *a* finger plays voice 2 notes softly on the downbeat, followed by the harmonized and heavily accented melody (voice 1) played with *i* and *m* on off-beats one-*and* two-*and*. The *i* and *m* fingers also play the harmonized notes on beat three-*and*, but that offbeat is unaccented, causing those notes to be heard as part of the voice 2 counter-figure. The fretted voice 1 notes are played staccato in contrast to the open string sound of voice 2. Those articulations together with the syncopation and the sharp contrast in volume create a unique texture—like an echo effect when played properly (voice 2 echoes voice 1). The bass (voice 3) is played at a dynamic level between the other two voices with a little pitch modulation on the dotted half notes—slowly phrasing a longer figure over the six measures that contrasts against the short, choppy repetition of voice 1.

There are situations in which the same finger or group of fingers plays consecutive notes with sharply contrasting volumes. In **Example 4**, *p* plays the long notes of the bass (voice 3), while fingers *i, m, a* play the chords. The chords are played softly on the downbeats (voice 2) and heavily accented on the offbeats (voice 1). This requires a continual and consistent alteration of pressure exerted by the same fingers on every eighth note to achieve a similar echo effect as in Example 2b (from earlier in this lesson). Experiment with articulations.

Ex. 2
Tuning: D A D G C E♭

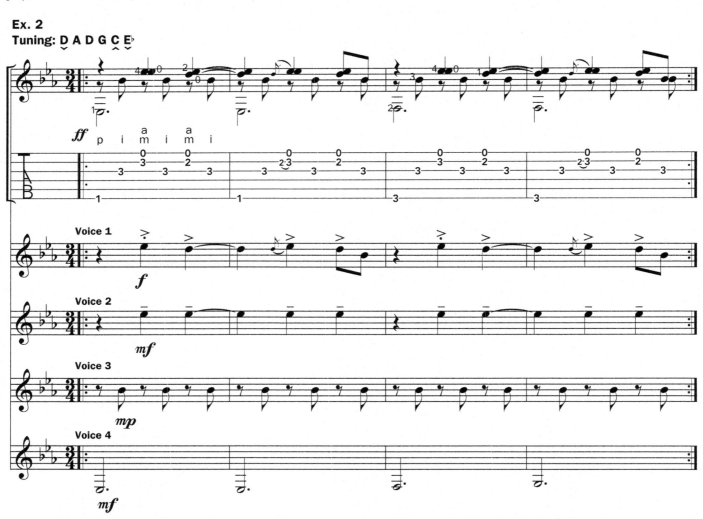

THE 3-D SOUND
Orchestration

Ex. 3
Tuning: D A D G C E♭

Ex. 4
Tuning: D A D G C E♭

THE ALEX DE GRASSI FINGERSTYLE GUITAR METHOD

In other situations, a pattern can be altered by moving the accent and/or the picking-hand fingering. In **Example 5** the accent stays on beat one-*and* of the first two measures, but the picking-hand fingering shifts from *a* in measure 1 to *m* in measure 2. The accents shift to the downbeat and the three-and in measure 3—both played with *a*. The accent in measure 4, also on the downbeat, is played with *m*. The inner voice (voice 2) in this passage is a little unusual. Consisting mostly of E♭ drone notes, voice 2 thickens the texture and adds some counterpoint by outlining a different rhythmic phrase.

Sequential Voices

Many arrangements do not use arpeggios or recognizable patterns like the previous examples. Different voices may come and go, follow one another sequentially, or merely function as a color or special effect. The sense of orchestration unfolds over time, throughout the course of a piece. **Example 6**, an excerpt from my composition "Deep at Night," has been elaborated from the original transcription to illustrate some of the finer points of phrasing and orchestration.

Ex. 5

THE 3-D SOUND
Orchestration

The melody (voice 1) has a lyrical, vocal quality that begins somewhat freely. Some of the melody notes are accented to punctuate the phrasing. Some notes (stems down) are sustained, creating a "sub-voice" consisting of key tones (voice 2) that creates a layered, overlapping effect in the way the melody is phrased.

The first bass note (voice 3, E♭), played softer than the melody, arrives on the downbeat of measure 2. It's repeated in measure 4 and then a still lower bass voice (voice 4) an octave below appears at the end of the measure and continues through measure 7. Voice 4 is played *tambor* on the strings very softly—unmuted and very close to the saddle. It has a pitch but functions more like a low drum in the distance. On the upbeat of measure 6 a slow reverse up-strum (see explanation below tab) consisting of a five-note harmonic chord (natural and artificial) adds yet another color (voice 5). In this short passage a combination of dynamics, accents, articulations, and timbre work together to suggest five instruments or voices.

Some of these voices, like the harmonics, only surface for special effect. Later in the piece, the rhythm gains momentum. This is emphasized by some slapped percussion bass notes in measures 12 and 13—perhaps suggesting the reappearance of a somewhat altered voice 4 *tambor* sound from measures 4–7. At beat three-*and* in measure 14, and again in measure 17, a brief return of the counter-melody or sub-voice (voice 2) answers the call of the melody line. Playing those lines somewhat softer or with a different timbre differentiates them from the main melody.

Beginning on the last eighth note of measure 20 and continuing through measure 22, a three-note chord melody answers the main melody. This could be thought of as yet another voice (voice 6) played by a chordal instrument (perhaps piano or harp). The main melody resumes on the upbeat of measure 23 played as the top voice of a full chord. It's almost as if the chordal voice 6 that entered in measure 20 is now supporting the melody. Finally, voice 5 reappears in measure 26 with two harmonics that seem to echo the last melody notes of the passage.

It's difficult to include in a guitar transcription all the possible articulations and expressions that give a performance depth and character. Some transcriptions are more detailed than others. Learning to recognize the possibilities inherent in a piece requires careful listening and some analysis. Working through short passages and testing different ways of interpreting the music, whether it's written or not, can also help you see the big picture. Learning to arrange and orchestrate what you play is an important step toward building a 3-D sound.

Ex. 6: "Deep at Night"
Tuning: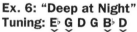

* Slap downstemmed notes softly with side of thumb near the saddle.

**Fret 4th and 5th strings with fretting hand. Extend picking hand i across all strings at 7th fret (and 7th fret of 5th string) and strum up with a as the picking hand sweeps across all six strings.

Acknowledgments

This book was a long time in the making and could not have been realized without the help and encouragement of many people. Thanks to my editors Jeffrey Rodgers and Dan Gabel for all their hard work, good judgment, and infinite patience. Thanks to Andrew DuBrock for working his Finale magic on all the music examples. Thanks to Hugh O'Connor, Adam Traum, and Barbara Summer for making it all look good. Thanks to Alison de Grassi for patiently listening and making suggestions. Thanks to all the guitarists who inspired me to go down that fingerstyle road: Bukka White, Mississippi John Hurt, Paul Simon, John Fahey, Robbie Basho, Leo Kottke, Bert Jansch, John Renbourn, Will Ackerman, and all the rest. Thank you to all my students for giving me the opportunity to road-test the material and exercises contained in this book. Finally, a very special thanks to David Lusterman for the opportunity to make the book a reality, and to John Stropes for his encouragement and scholarly devotion to all things fingerstyle.

About the Author

Alex de Grassi has been a unique voice in the world of acoustic guitar for over 30 years, and his innovative approach to composing and arranging for solo steel-string guitar has influenced a generation of players. From his first solo performances in coffeehouses and as a street musician to his engagements at Carnegie Hall, the Kennedy Center, and the Montreux Jazz Festival, de Grassi has followed his own vision and, in the process, helped to lay the foundation for contemporary fingerstyle guitar.

Inspired by American and British Isles folk and blues artists in his early teens, he soon expanded his musical pursuits to encompass classical, jazz, and world music. He has since become known for his evocative compositions and arrangements, innovative use of alternate tunings, and highly orchestrated sound.

De Grassi's 1978 debut solo guitar recording *Turning: Turning Back*, on the Windham Hill label, led *Downbeat Magazine* to declare, "De Grassi has mastered the art of playing melodies, countermelodies, harmonies, and intricate rhythms simultaneously. His touch is as exquisite as his lyricism, and his improvisational/compositional musical consciousness is as intricate as sparkling crystal." Of the *Slow Circle* album from 1979, *Guitar Player* magazine wrote, "De Grassi's solo steel-string guitar pieces resemble orchestral overtures more than mere songs." Those albums, along with *Southern Exposure* (1984) and his Grammy-nominated recording *The Water Garden* (1998), are considered classics of the genre. The *Wall Street* Journal has called his playing "flawless," and *Billboard* hails his "uncanny gift for melodic invention."

De Grassi has received commissions from Stringletter to compose a concerto for steel-string guitar, string quartet, and string orchestra (in collaboration with Quartet San Francisco leader and violinist Jeremy Cohen), and from the New York Guitar Festival to compose and perform live scores for the festival's Silent Films/Live Guitars series. Festival director David Spelman says, "Alex de Grassi is a treasure. . . . His technical wizardry as well as his vibrant and poetic music-making make him one of the most distinctive steel-string guitarists performing today."

De Grassi has recorded several instructional and concert videos with Mel Bay, Hal Leonard, and Homespun, and his guitar transcriptions have been published by Hal Leonard, Stropes Editions, Stringletter, and numerous guitar magazines. He has been a frequent guest teacher at the National Summer Guitar Workshop, the Interlochen Institute, Berklee School of Music, the Omega Institute, Crown of the Continent, Marin Community Music School, and the unique Fingerstyle Guitar Program at University of Wisconsin in Milwaukee. He lives in northern California.